Drifting north

Manchester University Press

Drifting north

Finding a sustainable future in Scotland's past

Dominic Hinde

MANCHESTER UNIVERSITY PRESS

The right of Dominic Hinde to be identified as the author of this work has been asserted in accordance with the Copyright, Designs and Patents Act 1988.

Published by Manchester University Press
Oxford Road, Manchester, M13 9PL

www.manchesteruniversitypress.co.uk

British Library Cataloguing-in-Publication Data
A catalogue record for this book is available from the British Library

ISBN   978 1 5261 7821 3   hardback

First published 2025

The publisher has no responsibility for the persistence or accuracy of URLs for any external or third-party internet websites referred to in this book, and does not guarantee that any content on such websites is, or will remain, accurate or appropriate.

EU authorised representative for GPSR:
Easy Access System Europe, Mustamäe tee 50, 10621 Tallinn, Estonia
gpsr.requests@easproject.com

Typeset
by New Best-set Typesetters Ltd

Contents

Prologue: a time of monsters

Without the story – in which everyone living, unborn and dead, participates – men are no more than bits of paper blown on the cold wind.

George Mackay Brown

It's hot. Hotter than I can ever remember here. It's late June and I'm standing on the beach on the east side of Loch Lomond with my dad in the evening light, looking across the surface of the water. There is a cloudless sky above the Luss Hills where they cave inwards and up into the steep cleft of Glen Douglas on the western shore. The spring green is turning brown as the summer makes itself felt, the gorse flowers gone and the heather yet to arrive, but then this year all bets seem off anyway. The pebbles on the beach are warm after weeks of baking in the sun, the shallows barely colder than the air. Smoke from disposable barbecues drifts across the horizon as the long Scottish twilight begins, turning the slopes of Ben Lomond malachite gold.

Dad is paddling, a baseball cap protecting his head from the sun and his trousers rolled up around his calves, with his shoes placed neatly on the beach. I pull my phone out to send the rest of the family a picture. My brother is in America, where he teaches in an elementary school and it is still early afternoon. In the chat a picture of the Chicago skyline appears, with wildfire smoke obscuring the skyscrapers. Scotland is warmer than usual, but the US and Canada are suffering. There is a heat dome over the continent and going outside has been declared dangerous for the elderly and young people as the particles drift on the breeze. The kids in my brother's Illinois school class hide behind sealed glass before being ferried home in the backs of air-conditioned cars. A few weeks later the hottest average day yet recorded on earth will be registered and confirmed by meteorologists.

Climate change was always there, at the edges. I was born in the late 1980s, when the first wisps of climate science were beginning to burrow into the collective consciousness. The six o'clock news was full of TV reports showing factory smokestacks and close-ups of car exhausts, and our school textbooks had crude diagrams showing the greenhouse effect alongside the hand-drawn cutaways of atoms and explanations of coastal erosion. It was a detail to note down. We were told that by the time we were adults it would all be solved through a calm marriage of politics and technology.

Twenty-five years on from that primary-school textbook I find myself in a lecture at the Ludwig Maximilian University in Munich, doodling with a pen on a notebook in a presentation I do not fully understand. I'm in a seminar room at an environmental research institute watching another academic talk about the multiplication effects of atmospheric carbon, surrounded by students and researchers.

I'd moved back to Germany after a decade away, picking up where I left off aged 21 as a trainee reporter in Berlin, to write a book on climate change as a fellow at the Institute. All of us brought something to the table: sociologists, geographers, chemists, historians and ecologists rubbing shoulders with literature experts and science writers. The logic was that somewhere in that mass of knowledge was a solution to the biggest problem of them all.

Every few weeks we would leave our desks behind to socialise, heading to the open-air restaurants and beer gardens in the English Garden opposite on the banks of the River Isar. The English Garden is where Thomas Mann's novella *Death in Venice* begins, where his burned-out and weary protagonist hallucinates visions of a primordial landscape full of steaming vegetation and swamp against the neatly landscaped contours of the park as the first stage in a slow and inevitable descent. In the background lurks the spectre of a world war. It's an apt place for a group of climate researchers to congregate.

The park itself is a pastoral dreamscape, sculpted from the flood plain of the river and dotted with temples and ornamental bridges under the domes of the Munich Altstadt. We sit by the Chinese Tower as the light begins to fade and the neat lawns recede into blackness, voices trailing off into the dark. I need to write, so I make my excuses to get home and work on the book. I climb onto my bike and head west along the river, to my apartment by the railway bridge in the Isarvorstadt, the high Alps taking the last of the sunlight for themselves as I leave the gravel of the park behind me and ride onto the tarmac streets.

Taxis crowd the cycle lane in the square, waiting to pick up weekday drinkers looking for home and bringing tourists out to replace them. There is electricity in the breeze, a mountain thunderstorm threatening to roll in from Switzerland, charged by the warm vapour rising from the lakes of the Bavarian Oberland. The city feels wired and ready to blow, and as I pedal the charged air skirts my face. My mind wanders from the road to the desk at home.

Then, black.

I wake up looking at a sky turning slowly with the energy of the coming storm. Faces over me. There are three, five, maybe? I'm no longer on the bike. My first thought is for the bag containing my computer and my research notes. My left cheek is flat on the ground and I have landed on my jaw, with the rest of me coming down behind it like a train hitting the buffers. The bike itself is improbably far away, lying on the cobbles with a bent handlebar and a broken cargo tray.

Someone hands me a plastic bottle and I sit up, spitting bloody water onto the ground. I ask how long I've been out. A few seconds, they say, maybe more. Nobody caught the whole thing, but I'd hit a blind kerb and gone straight over. The impact traced a line that began at the left corner of my mouth and continued through to a point under my right ear. In rehab therapy a year later the therapist would make me lie on the carpet of the consultation room in the same position, imagining the kinetic energy as it is dissipated through the white matter of my brain.

I refuse an ambulance, make three phone calls I can't remember, and walk to the casualty admissions of the hospital on my own. The duty registrar parks me in a corner like a tourist in the drunk tank and sends me away at midnight, telling me I'm fine. A week later I almost pass out while speaking to a class at the university.

I tell myself I'm tired and go and sit by the river to rest. Swollen by the summer storm water, the Isar should be a torrent racing down through the sluices and weirs, but it doesn't flow. Instead, buildings move from right to left like a zoetrope, wound by an unseen hand along a moving backscene. Everyone around me casually ignores the liquid buildings and solid water, clinking bottles of beer on the rocks or jumping in to be carried by the current to the next bridge. I have been locked out of reality.

Post-concussion syndrome is a functional brain disorder that presents in patients with neurological trauma, often long after the initial damage has begun to heal. It is a syndrome because nobody understands fully how and why it happens, and is diagnosed based on observation of symptoms rather than any clear understandings of its causes. It disrupts vision, balance, speech and memory, and patients often report emotional dysregulation and manic thoughts as the brain tries to make sense of itself. The connective tissue that binds the brain together is corrupted, forcing the mind to make new connections and reroute old ones to reinvent the person that holds them. It often gets worse before getting better, and a week after the collapse I find I can't even look at a computer screen without the right side of my body seizing up.

My tongue tastes cold metal whenever I see bright lights, and the world moves with the detached roughness of a film rendered with the wrong frame rate. Any attempt to work on my laptop brings on a racing heartbeat and severe pain that begins in my right jaw and slowly leaches through one half of my body. The idea of writing anything, let alone the book I am working on, begins to fade as the full horror sets in. Broken legs and faulty organs can be patched and cast, transplanted and bypassed. Brain trauma makes you a hostage in your own life.

Eight months after waking up on the street I am back home in Scotland and beginning to show signs of improvement, when suddenly there are news reports of an outbreak of virulent flu in central China. It seems improbable until suddenly it isn't, and hospital wards fill up with acutely sick people. The TV shows mass graves being dug in preparation for the anticipated deaths; the world hangs on a thread of indecision. Futures are cancelled and new ones are hastily assembled, and we wait. People begin to report strange symptoms – chronic fatigue, cognitive impairment, depression and a constant gasping for oxygen as if the air around were suddenly thick with smoke. After about eight weeks I catch it and my condition begins to worsen again.

COVID-19 is an example of what philosophers of science call hyperobjects, things that touch everyone and everything but which are too big to see on their own. Viruses are invisible and strange, half alive and so numerous that if we could see them it would radically change our understanding of the world as we move through it. Like the bacteria on every surface and floating in the air, we sense them only when they make themselves felt, yet without them life as we know it would cease to exist.

We think we live in a world steered by politicians and economists, by media narratives and technological innovation and stock markets, but we rest in a web of microorganisms, chemical compounds and unseen interactions. Even our bodies are not single entities but assemblages of life. We are hybrid creatures, all of us a multitude.

Climate change is a hyperobject too, impossible to touch or see at will but embedded in every facet of life and reaching into the fabric of our existence. Viruses move invisibly through the air, but the air moves invisibly as well. A cocktail of atmospheric gases propelled by the exchange of heat, the air in our lungs is part of an immeasurably huge problem that is as deadly as the viruses it carries. Hyperobjects transcend borders and stretch their tendrils through the connective tissue of the modern world, a web of movement, consumption, growth and collapse, of bacteria and viruses, greenhouse gases and dust particles circulating invisibly before our eyes and transforming the globe and us in unimaginable ways. Occasionally we see flashes of this shadow-world, fleeting glimpses that become fully formed figures for moments at a time, but we can never see the whole thing at once.

We made climate change and we made the coronavirus, not intentionally but in the acceleration of energy, life, mobility and connection that began with the Industrial Revolution and continues today. We built a modernity always faster and more violent until one day viruses mutated in central China were able to ride in warm bodies chewing microwaved food in plastic tubs, in aeroplanes powered by the remains of long-dead plants and animals through a warming atmosphere across the globe.

We live in an age of monsters moulded from the flows of the modern life and given life by indecision, denial and indifference, sitting at our shoulder every day. All monsters have a story, and the story of climate change is the story of the modern world, of jet planes and steam engines, progress and regress, and of a planet we have remade that is also remaking us.

I teach at the University of Glasgow, in the Sociology department in a crumbling concrete building that has borne the worst of half a century of Scottish winter storms. Scotland is a place where the climate giant comes into clearer view, and not just because of the weather. Home to one of the world's earliest large-scale coalfields, birthplace of the modern steam engine, foundational to market capitalism and, in a Faustian pact with an oil industry that has promised much and delivered far less, Scotland helped to build the modern world and now lives in its ruins. It is also my home, and each time I come back to it I see it differently.

It says 'sociologist' on my office door but that isn't the whole story. I was, for a fair while, a foreign journalist, and then I became a media researcher. I came late to sociology, arriving the long way round after realising that I was happiest doing fieldwork rather than kicking the skirting board in an office, and that journalism was really a kind of anthropology of the extreme present.

When people ask what I do I often struggle to answer, but the fundamental elements of it are that I record people on a little radio microphone and use what they say to try and make sense of the world, to put flesh on the bones of reality. That's the sum total of my talent and ambition. The common thread is to resist the constant pressure to live in smaller worlds and to make them bigger for other people too. Climate change desperately needs us all to live bigger lives than our own.

Three years on from the warm night in Munich I am at my desk trying to pick through notes that had been waiting for me to be well enough to deal with them. The initial book is long gone. Some of the scribbles barely make sense at all; others are hopelessly outdated, overtaken by events and new climate data. The doctors have warned me about overexertion. I'm told to limit foreign trips and stay at home as much as I can. COVID-19 has hit me three times like a sledgehammer, bringing new complications.

Chronic illness brings chronic boredom, and after three years of being a half-person I was desperate to make my world bigger. My radio mic was unused and gathering dust on the office shelf, so I took it down and plugged in my headphones to see what was on there. It was an old memory card, voices from long ago – Iceland, Estonia, Venice, Stockholm and Brazil. I wipe it and put in new batteries. I'm ready to start travelling and writing again, claiming back the self I thought I'd lost in the Munich hospital.

Unexpectedly, I've had an email from a publisher. We talk about ideas as I leaf through the notebooks. For the first time in a long while I feel excited by work. On the front page of one of them is a hand-scribbled list of places where climate change is making itself felt. I rule out the long haul and focus on what I can do with a misfiring body, marking off the names from the top of Shetland to the English border. I need to be within a day's travel of Glasgow and Scotland's health service in case I have a seizure. If I can't go out into the world I will go and find it in Scotland.

There's a knock at my office door. It's Dad, appearing with two cups of coffee picked up on his way from the Subway station. I used to visit him at work quite a bit, walking the floor of the railway workshops where the ballast under the track was black with diesel oil and engine lubricant and the sheds thick with fumes. This is the first time he's ever been to see me. Even after I finished my PhD he'd email me job adverts for driving positions on the railway, which pay better per hour than either academia or journalism.

Dad sits on the small office sofa where I curl up when I'm hit by fog or fatigue and sleep it off. I'm packing for my first few forays onto the road, the place full of holdalls and kit waiting to be stowed in the boot of an ancient Honda hatchback bought for £2,000 cash and a promise to be kind to it. We drink our coffee and get in the car, unsure where we are headed; I suggest taking him up to Loch Lomond in the passenger seat, to the beaches of the national park. In the disquieting heat we head north, overtaking tourists on the road through Strathblane out of Glasgow with the hills rising on either side, pulling us towards the mountains proper.

We stand there on the shores of Loch Lomond, the familiar foil tray of emergency brain medication nestling comfortingly between the fingers in my pocket. As I watch Dad in the shallows, I think about the wildfires burning in North

America and my brother behind plate glass staring out at skyscrapers in the haze, about the sunset in the English Garden and the looming spectre of a world torn apart. The wildfire smoke will drift across the Atlantic and cause vivid sunsets in Scotland for a few days afterwards. Heat rises from the loch into the atmosphere as monsters stir in the depths and the contours of the Highland peaks burn black in the distance.

1

In the carbon museum

I pick Ewan up in the Honda and we roll through the eastern suburbs of Glasgow and out into Lanarkshire. The car fan blows the unadulterated fossil heat of the engine over the dashboard and onto the damp windscreen, drowning out the traffic reports from BBC Radio Scotland on the outdated FM stereo. The Clyde Valley is almost always wet. My local mechanic says a car will rust through twice as quickly in the west of Scotland as in the east, so by the time you finish paying off the loan you are sitting in a pile of scrap metal.

We loop through slip roads and dual carriageways and circle up past the Celtic FC stadium fans call Paradise, on the old road east from the days before the motorway was cut through the wet soil of the watershed between the Atlantic and North Sea. Football in Glasgow is not just dominated by religion; it *is* religion, a faith that found its people in the exploding population of the late 1800s as the city became one of the most important industrial centres on earth.

Until the 1700s the higher ground immediately east of Glasgow was still bucolic farmland, rolling green fields and pockets of woods that stretched out to open moors across the spine of Scotland. It was known as the Monklands after the monasteries that had been granted the land in the 1100s. The monks mined coal from shallow seams close to the surface, until the Church had its assets confiscated in the Scottish Reformation in a deliberate move to undermine Catholic power. Scotland became a staunchly Protestant country that eagerly exported its faith as well as its coal around the world as part of the civilising impulse of empire. You can tell whether Scots colonised a country by counting the Presbyterian chapels and the gravestones outside, but also the rusting steam engines in faded museums with the names of Glasgow factories on their builder's plate.

Ewan works down from me in the corridors of the University of Glasgow and teaches energy history. We'd first met on the football terraces on the east coast, and by chance ended up working at Glasgow together. Our conversation fluctuates between the history of fossil energy and the continued ability of Hibernian Football Club to snatch defeat from the jaws of victory. He has an encyclopaedic knowledge of the Lanarkshire coalfields, towns and union men, mining disasters and output statistics. In his day job he gathers the memories of former mineworkers and memorialises the last days of an industry that lasted two centuries and changed the face of the earth.

I'd sought him out, asking if he could give me a tour of the towns of the coal belt in return for me doing the driving, and he'd said yes. It was him who suggested following the course of the old coal canal to Glasgow's east end, where James Watt, an instrument maker at the university, had first come up with the condensing steam engine that helped build an empire based on coal power. Watt's design led to trains, steamships and industrial manufacturing on a scale never seen before. The British Empire was built on iron and fossil energy and Glasgow was at the heart of it.

Fundamentally climate change is a deep story of energy, of our thirst for it, and of wood, coal, oil and gas. It is a story that transcends our own lifetimes, but which in the entire history of the earth is just the blink of an eye, a few hundred years when the modern world was made and then unmade by its own hand.

We're chasing waterfalls, or rather one in particular, behind which lurk climate monsters. The waterfall in question is also James Watt's creation, channelling a natural river into the canal cut where it begins just outside the town of Airdrie. Suddenly mines pumped by steam engines could take coal to factories and foundries, where it was burned to unleash the energy locked inside at a previously unimaginable pace, and the waterfall is at the source of it all.

When we find it it's less impressive than expected, a modest drop from the natural river into the flat bed of the canal. A few dog owners amble in the drizzle, walking the path on the now impassable waterway, which has not seen a boat since the 1950s. The canal was dug out by hundreds of human hands, only to be usurped by the trains it helped fuel.

As the rain worsens we head uphill on foot, back towards the car, and cut through former mining villages and across the remains of the Monkland Colliery. Here there is only scrub and the odd stray length of iron rail hiding in the ivy, the pits sealed and winding gear demolished. As we go, Ewan reels off statistics about the number of pits and the failed attempts at retraining miners to make electronics in a Korean-owned factory down the road.

On the other side of the abandoned mine we find the latest example of international investment, a branch of Starbucks on a retail park next to the football stadium in Airdrie. Teenagers sip iced lattes and hatchbacks styled to look like 4x4s roll into the drive-through to pick up cupcakes and flat whites via lowered windows. Even though car engines have become more efficient due to environmental regulations, the average car has grown bigger and bigger, so they still consume huge amounts of fuel. It's a winning strategy from car makers and oil companies, always up-selling for more horsepower and legroom.

Airdrie is the new post-industrial Scotland of retail parks and innovation zones, of cars bought on credit and newbuild suburbs designed to make people feel rich by tying them to lifetime mortgages and finance plans. The industrial estates across the motorway that flashes past house container terminals and logistics centres, bringing in things made elsewhere to be sent somewhere else again.

A few miles away is an industrial heritage park where visitors can see re-creations of a local mining village and learn about the history of North Lanarkshire. Its halls are filled with silent steam engines and redundant coalface equipment, the café with screaming children and pensioners hiding from the weather. The whole of Scotland often feels like a living museum, populated by people telling stories about the past to anyone who will listen. History sells – in a world of disconnection and isolation there is an appetite for some kind of meaningful and structured encounter with a better past, real or imagined. People think that historians are curators of immutable facts and artefacts dredged from archives and muddy fields, but history is really an archaeology of the present, digging up explanations for our current predicaments. Museums are a form of public memory that help to smooth out the process.

I ask Ewan for a soundbite to test the microphone as he sips on his coffee. The plan had been to try and talk to anyone local about Airdrie and coal, but the weather has driven most people indoors and the teenagers around us have probably never used the stuff, let alone dug it. He takes off his glasses and rubs them on his coat, removing the condensation.

He starts, then stops again. After some thought the words come out: 'History is understandings of the past, mediated by individual memories and absorbed through collective understanding.'

He takes another breath.

'And that people use to help them navigate their current contexts.' He moves to say more before deciding the first go was enough.

'That's as good as I can do.'

Memory is fallible, and how we remember has implications for what we do. When your mind isn't working properly it throws your sense of self into chaos as you drift along, desperately trying to find something solid to grip. Climate change is no different, as we scrape around for a solid future, but it reaches further back and forwards than any single life by a measure of ten generations.

When I'd first explained my idea to go to the Monklands, Ewan had replied with a glib 'sounds decent'. It was not long before Glasgow was due to host the United Nations' annual climate-change negotiations, and Scotland was going through one of the occasional phases when the rest of the world turns its head in our direction. Wandering the hallways of the climate summit in a fugue state, I was unsure whether I was overwhelmed by illness or the sheer scale of the challenge laid out in front of me in the exhibition halls. I was a delegate at a trade expo hawking the future of civilisation: smart tech, carbon credits, machines that suck greenhouse gases from the air, nuclear reactors, energy-neutral houses and hydrogen plants.

Each UN session is a bigger circus. I know a veteran environmental journalist who attended the first climate COP in the early 1990s, when it was just a smattering of activists and technocrats locked in a hotel complex to debate the implications of the studies emerging from the world's universities and governments. Nobody was trying to make money out of it. The circus came after, when it became clear that climate change was going to cost a lot to fix.

We give up looking for people in Airdrie and we pick up the car so I can drop Ewan back home as the rain comes in for another pass, finding nobody and nothing but some abandoned shopping trolleys on our way out of town. The emptiness of the streets is a story in itself, as coal villages have morphed into linear motorway satellite towns. People are either at home or elsewhere, moving from house to car and work before coming back again through streets that used to be full of people walking to pitheads and workshops.

This is the side of Scotland you never see in the government press releases, tourist pictures or investment prospectuses. There is an implicitly agreed story about the virtuous little nation at the top of the world that invented carbon capitalism and then emerged from the doldrums to take a leading role in the fight against climate change and global injustice. The government talks without irony about Brand Scotland, positioning us as whatever the world wishes we were. At Edinburgh's main railway station there used to be an advertisement hoarding that greeted you off the train from London – *Welcome to the best small country in the world*, it said, in text eight feet high. Maybe it seemed true for a while, or at least we could convince ourselves. Memory is an unreliable friend.

Coal came to an end in Lanarkshire because the pits were exhausted and the world moved on. The carbon age is coming to an end because it has to if we are going to survive, even though there is plenty of coal left to mine. The consequences of continuing to rely on coal and oil are far worse than anything humanity has collectively experienced before.

* * *

It's springtime and I'm in a mining town without any mines and a miners' club without any miners, an hour down the motorway from Glasgow. Ewan has sent me here, to a place where the beginning and the end of the carbon age join together.

Coalburn is a community of a few hundred, a fold in the hills of South Lanarkshire where the high moors that separate Scotland and England begin. An isolated industrial village just out of sight beyond the motorway crash barriers, before coal, Coalburn did not exist. After coal it hangs on, trying to find a purpose in a world that has passed it by. Mines around Coalburn gouged carbon from the earth for burning for almost three hundred years – a few houses became a shanty town and finally a model community.

Coal was dirty but it built a miniature welfare state; schools, social clubs, shops and parks all sprang from the mines. As well as being an early deep mine, Coalburn was also one of the last places in Britain where coal was pulled out of the ground. Above the village, slag heaps create miniature mountains and give 360-degree views of a carbon museum for anyone with the energy to climb the 40-degree slopes. From the top you can also see the new economy: wind turbines, solar farms and the grey bulk of industrial-battery warehouses. Coalburn is a metaphor too good to be true, a new low-carbon powerhouse literally built on the ashes of the old.

Mick ushers me into his office in the back rooms of the miners' club. His desk is in a modern annexe that doubles as a community café and hub, with a small museum attached. He reminds me of a lower-league football manager who should have quit long ago hanging on for the love of the game, but instead of a tactics board on the wall Mick has a huge map of the glen dotted with pins. Each one marks a new energy project.

Mick is one of the last of a generation of working-class men in public life who got there through trade unions and the Labour Party. He's been a miner, a local councillor, and now the custodian of Coalburn's carbon museum. Surrounded by files and stacks of paper, I have to sit fully straight to see him over the wall of documentation that takes up most of a desk, which in turn takes up most of the office. He starts talking before I can even turn on the microphone.

What does another researcher want from him? He's spoken to so many and told them much the same. Every interview I do comes with a little information sheet approved by a university ethics committee, giving a prosaic and easy-to-understand explanation of the fieldwork that does not really do justice to the richness of the reality it is chasing. I try and reassure Mick that this is of some kind of larger social benefit.

Plenty of books are written about the death of industrial Scotland and government reports issued. Money is dished out for university studies, for interpretation displays and commemorative statues, and politicians make overtures towards honouring working class memory. Commemoration can be a comforting place to live without moving on, though. Mourning the past does not automatically make the future.

Mick spent most of his career handling coal, and he speaks like a man who knows the world turns on the arrival and departure of loaded trains and trucks and the people who make it happen. I say I'm not writing another history, nor am I a journalist looking for a quick story, at least not any more. It's about trying to work out the moment we are in before it is too late. What does it mean to be here in these few years when everything changes?

Our conversation is interrupted by a cash machine in the corner beeping into life and whirring as someone takes out notes on the street. We sit awkwardly in silence until it is finished dispensing money, like two men who have run out of conversation at a party. Radio mics are so sensitive that the whirr of a bank machine or the screech of a power drill in the next building can ruin a recording. My interviews are full of the distant sounds of truck engines, passing helicopters and clanking dishes, wind turbines, anchor chains and the laboured breathing of COVID-19-hit lungs.

The banks won't put a cash machine in the village as it isn't profitable for them, so the miners' welfare had one installed. Every so often the Scottish local press is peppered with stories of gangs driving diggers into ATMs and scooping them out of the wall before getting to work with power saws and welding torches. It's a big crime in a small town, a pathway to unimaginable riches within a small horizon.

Coalburn reminds me of the decimated coal towns of West Virginia in the US, where I'd once interviewed a man like Mick for a radio documentary, a local mayor with a gun in his desk drawer and a *Coal State* numberplate on his SUV. The fog hangs in the long valleys of Appalachia in the same way it clouds the glens of southern Scotland. The difference in Scotland is that coal never hitched its wagon to God, jingoism and kamikaze capitalism like it did in America. In that same town I'd met victims of the opioid epidemic sweeping the US rust belt unable to pay for rehab programmes, scratching around for cash jobs. In the empty mills and factories of the Upper Potomac Valley there was nobody for company but the vultures high above.

Mick talks of the usual things people past sixty talk about – children and grandchildren, friends and neighbours who have cancer or been hospitalised by COVID, and the scandals in the Scottish government that rumble on. He is as disenchanted by politics as everyone else. His Labour Party membership was terminated a while ago. He has firm opinions on the new class of professional politicians that have risen up since Scotland regained its own parliament, many on a conveyor from university to election, propelled by powerful party machines and the sincere belief they are born to lead.

Old, working-class Scotland is not always glamorous but it is a place of habitual hospitality. Mick refuses to let me pay for lunch and says I can have any toasted sandwich of my choice. The ham-and-cheese melt arrives with some crisps and coleslaw on the side, and I'm glad for the food. I'm starting to feel dizzy, and the salt and fat go straight to my brain. Mick seems to register that I'm drifting and he gestures outside towards his car. 'I'll drive', he says. I wipe my mouth and we pull out of the car park in a loop around the head of the village. By one of the warehouses at the back of town we branch off onto a rumbling concrete service road and start to gain height.

These roads were originally built for the opencast mines that tore the last of the viable coal seams from the ground above Coalburn. Coal mining took place here for so long that when the excavators were ripping the surface seams in the 1990s they uncovered 200-year-old drift mines with four-foot ceilings and wooden props. Where men once pushed handcarts and chipped away with pickaxes, the excavators simply obliterated everything in their path with their hydraulic arms and diesel power units. The pre-cast slabs stabilised the ground to support the weight of loaded trucks bringing the raw coal to the crushing plant, before being dropped into coal wagons and transported to thermal power stations in a fine powder. Mick worked for a long time checking the quality of the coal as it was loaded into the hoppers. Coalburn kept Scotland warm and well-lit through many long winters.

'Some of the stuff they used to send down was rubbish and you'd send it back', he tells me from the driver's seat. 'But it was good coal.' He isn't the first former miner to remind me that they kept the country going. It is one of the things that gave coal work meaning.

At first glance the landscape around the road is wild moorland, spruce trees and scrub stretching up to the horizon – the restoration workers have done a good job. If you follow the contours of the ground you can see the outline of the pits, technically still industrial land and ripe for development. It's what makes Coalburn a perfect place to roll out turbines and photovoltaics, hitching them to the grid through high-capacity substations in the shadow of the motorway.

Mick stops the car so I can clearly see the turbines, high as office blocks on top of the former strip mine. Up the glen there is another new solar array waiting to be switched on. By the time the mines closed they were in private hands, and the land passed to investors, who now sublet patches to different renewables companies.

'Have you seen all you need to?' he asks, turning the car on one of the loading pads as trucks carrying pre-mixed concrete rumble past to the construction sites up-valley. Coalburn is a place where the past and the future mingle, the solar parks and turbines springing up above the heaps of coal waste and the mining cottages. There is a fortune hidden in the hills, a current moving down the glen and out into the world, where it commands a high price.

I leave Mick to his work and thank him again. I have the slightly detached sense of foreboding that comes whenever my brain is about to go through a bad patch, a feeling of being distant from my own actions and the people around me. Climbing back into my car, I fumble around the glove box until I find the packet of medication that helps head off the haze working outwards from my right temple, then pull back out towards the motorway. One of my PhD students lives just across the border with England, and they've asked me to swing by for a cup of tea by the fire to meet their new baby – a warm room in a cold house heated with a wood stove. Gas prices are so steep that central heating is an invitation to bankruptcy.

I check the recordings and stash the mic in the back seat, pushing the car up and on.

2

Caol abhainn/the narrow river

Energy can be neither created nor destroyed. This is the first law of thermodynamics. The synaptic sparks in our bodies and the chemical exchanges that move our muscles and give us consciousness were once elsewhere. They were solar rays, prehistoric trees, coal seams, the spin of a steam turbine and the heat of millions of bulbs and electric heaters. The glow of televisions hits the photoreceptors of the eye and sends more electric signals surging down the optic nerve, until finally we experience the world in colour. We smell rising and falling air as the photons of the sun warm our skin, all fed to a brain maintained at an optimal temperature of 38.5 degrees Celsius by a system of electrical feedback loops that carefully regulate the temperature of the body. We are constellations of hydrocarbons animated by electricity, exchanging energy with the world around us.

We only experience heat energy within a tiny window of liveability on the surface of a wet sphere bound by a thin atmosphere. What we know as temperature is highly subjective. Hot for some things is cool for others, and the reference point for zero on the Celsius scale is the freezing point of water, a simple compound of hydrogen and oxygen that is so common and vital to our existence that it forms the basis of how we imagine heat itself. It freezes at zero and boils at one hundred, facts drummed into us from childhood so that we know not to plunge our hands into bubbling water or go outside without a coat when the air grips the railings and turns white.

Humans can live in a temperature range between 16 and 32 degrees Celsius without too much trouble. Any lower and we begin to lose heat too rapidly to function, any higher and we begin to struggle to get rid of the excess energy. The actual range of temperatures in the universe is almost inconceivable. The interior of a nuclear reactor burns at a range from 400 degrees to just under 1,000, depending on type, but the nuclear reactions in the sun give it a core temperature of 15 million Celsius. The universe as a whole has an ambient temperature of -270, getting colder all the time as heat continues to dissipate. We are a little damp, warm point in a cold universe interrupted by the violent heat of stars, where water can be liquid and where the atmosphere provides a stable regulation system for trillions of organisms. Hot on earth is nothing compared to the hottest points of the universe, and cold on earth can never come close to the barren solitude of the interstellar expanse, where the temperature pushes towards heat death and thermodynamic equilibrium. Climate change on earth is a footnote in existence, but an important one for the people who live on the planet.

Two peregrine falcons have taken up residence in the University of Glasgow's Gothic bell tower. These birds are the fastest animals on earth, with hearts that beat up to 900 times a minute, providing oxygen to wing muscles that beat 4 times a second and push them through the air and out above the city. They can attack at a speed of 200 miles an hour, using gravity to accelerate to a velocity where their prey is killed by the impact. Watching peregrines in flight is an exercise in the use and conservation of energy. They rise quickly, before soaring on air currents as they scan the airspace below. When they identify prey they pump their wings and use their feathers like the aerofoils of guided missiles. They are a perfect marriage of speed and form, hypnotic above the slate roofs of the campus.

I'm sat on the steps outside the university chapel, in a quad called Professors' Square next to the stone edifice of the main university building, watching the birds loop out and back in search of food. Before the university exploded in size tenured professors would be given townhouses here as part of their appointment, hosting students in their private studies. On the wall next to one of the doorways is a blue plaque bearing the name not of James Watt but another famous son of the university: Lord Kelvin, godfather of thermodynamics.

Kelvin was born William Thomson in an Ireland that was still part of the UK in 1824. He slotted into a world of engineering and science that had grown in lockstep with the expansion of the British Empire, and was enrolled at the University of Glasgow for basic study after the family relocated from Belfast following his father's appointment as Professor of Mathematics.

Kelvin would become synonymous with the university, thanks to his work on the nascent science of heat and energy, and Glasgow would become synonymous with cutting-edge physics and engineering for a century afterwards. His immortality was assured when his name was formally adopted as the unit of measurement for absolute temperature he had pioneered. In 1848 Kelvin suggested a temperature scale that was based not on the observed properties of water but on the measurement of heat energy itself. At zero Kelvin nothing moves, nothing warms, and the universe is a cold, dead place.

British political tradition lets appointees to the House of Lords choose their title, and when Thomson became Lord Kelvin he took the name of the valley in the shadow of the university on the city's western edge. A fluke of geography and history mean that not only the Kelvin scale, but things as diverse as a starship in the *Star Trek* universe, the protagonist in Stanislaw Łem's science fiction classic *Solaris* and a range of hills on the moon all carry the name of a fairly insignificant river running from the foot of Scotland's Campsie Fells into the Clyde Valley. The name itself most likely comes from the Gaelic *caol abhainn*, meaning narrow river. For its final few miles the River Kelvin plunges down through a narrow gorge past the Victorian edifice of the university and the landscaped avenues of Kelvingrove Park.

Every degree of global temperature rise means adding more energy to a semi-closed system, further disturbing the fragile equilibrium that has seen us through the last few million years. What we call weather is the flow of energy around us, transforming water from gas to liquid to solid and back again, and of temperature fluctuations pushing winds around the globe. Climate change is a system losing its rhythm, overcharged and unable to self-regulate as more and more heat becomes trapped in the atmosphere. Thermodynamics means that more energy leads to more movement, and more movement means atmospheric violence.

Kelvin would have been able to walk from his house on Professors' Square to the university bell tower and gaze out over a burning twilight of home fires, steam locomotives, factory furnaces and steamships fuelled by coal ripped from the seams around the city. The sandstone of the Victorian campus was stained soot-black. The poet W. H. Auden described the Clyde valley furnaces as giant chessmen set on the flat plain, burning through the night and casting a glow over the contours of the land in the absence of the sun. Immediately in front of the university the river loops around the perimeter fence, and on the other side of the water is the Kelvingrove Museum, a red fantasy edifice styled on a Spanish cathedral with hints of the British Raj. Intended to showcase Glasgow's status as a centre of the arts and sciences at the height of British power, the museum speaks to a time when Glasgow's elite were rich enough to buy up artefacts and paintings for municipal and private collections, or in some cases just to take them without consent from Britain's colonies.

It was under the vaulted ceilings of the museum that heads of government and state mingled during the UN climate summit when it came to Glasgow, whilst the rest of us were kettled outside behind steel riot railings. There were snipers on the rooftops and sniffer dogs on the streets, hunting for explosives. I was chucked out of a gallery where I was giving a talk and told to go home by Metropolitan Police officers who closed down the neighbourhood without warning. Behind the barriers starstruck Glaswegians jostled with protesters to catch glimpses of the President of the United States and the Prime Minister. When the canapés had been eaten and the Glasgow summit finished it was hailed as a major breakthrough, with countries agreeing to get rid of coal power in the long term to try and keep the world to 1.5 degrees of warming above pre-industrial levels.

They failed.

In 2024 the European Union's climate monitoring service confirmed that warming had exceeded 1.5 degrees Celsius worldwide across an entire year for the first time. All emissions scenarios based on current technologies and development show us breaking through the two-degree barrier. We are starting the race against climate change half a century too late.

Kelvin attempted to convince his fellow engineers to move on from coal to wind, which, he claimed, 'is a natural force which is practically inexhaustible, and which can be utilised without any consumption of fuel or production of smoke'. His pleas fell on deaf ears, and instead the world lost a hundred years of progress in wind technology, becoming ever more adept at finding and extracting coal and oil. Since I was born more carbon has been pumped into the atmosphere than in the hundred years prior.

Sat in my university office, listening back to people I have interviewed on the road, it seems overwhelming. For all the helpful talk of new wind farms and electric cars, the reality of the present sits in the margins. In front of me, Blu-Tacked to the wall, is a mess of printouts and lists: UN climate forecasts, government policy reports, and a cli-fi novel with the tell-tale ring of a coffee mug on the cover. On a chart I have colour-coded the climate emissions pathways showing different scenarios for the next hundred years, some liveable, some catastrophic.

Sea-level rises, heatwaves, extreme weather events, food shortages and resource conflicts are already beginning to seep into our everyday lives. The university has declared a climate emergency, but words are no more effective against climate change than thoughts and prayers in the face of violence. The recordings on the microphone are slow laments, disembodied voices each articulating a place and an experience. They are mostly people genuinely trying to do the right thing, working with what is in front of them in a compromised world.

One of the sound files is marked *Jaime.wav* with a date attached – May 2024. Jaime is a professor of Environmental and climate science and head of the university's Centre for Sustainable Solutions, Glasgow's attempt to marshal the forces of academia against the climate crisis. She's from the US, with the slightly adjusted accent of Americans and Canadians in Scotland that switches out the colloquialisms and the everyday words for the Scottish equivalents as the vowels track back east across the Atlantic. It's not unusual for long-time residents to be mistaken for Irish.

Her office is a minute from mine, down a set of particularly dangerous steps plastered with posters for communist meetings and opportunistic graffiti. Someone has pasted up a poster from *This is Rigged*, the anti-oil activist network that has taken root on campus and been recruiting from an angry and politicised student population.

Jaime trained as a climate scientist, specialising in paleoclimatology. Paleoclimatologists use fossils to build simulations of the climate going back millions of years, including the last time the earth went through a greenhouse phase similar to today, 55 million years ago. The university was founded in 1451, in the crossover between what climate scientists call the Medieval Warm Period and the Little Ice Age. The Medieval Warm Period seems to have been highly localised to Northern Europe, but it remains a favourite of climate deniers who want to pass off the current atmospheric crisis as another round of the same micro-effects. The Little Ice Age that came after was only a minor hiccup in the global climate record compared to where we are now. The unprecedented upward shifts in global temperature since the Industrial Revolution and the Second World War are like nothing human eyes have ever seen.

Now and then quirks of the seminar timetable mean I end up teaching in the rooms at the back of the university zoology museum, where the inhuman faces of dinosaurs and extinct megafauna stare back through glass eyes from glass display cases. We have previously had five mass extinctions on earth and are currently undergoing a sixth, which we may or may not yet be part of. In a million years there will be human fossils, made up of us, but also our plastics and reinforced concrete, crushed and buried as a record of a brief flash of earth history. Each extinction is not just a story of one animal failing to adapt, but of the collapse of a whole biome that would have seemed inconceivable had there been any brain big enough to witness it.

'Are there time periods in the past that can serve as analogues to what will happen in the future?' Jaime asks me rhetorically on the recording. We know there are, and over the last quarter-century climate science has gone faster and further in its quest to understand what life on a greenhouse earth might be like. Warmer seas, forests turning to grasslands, invasive species, wildfires, flooding and rising sea levels. What we know from past extinctions is that more complex life suffers. Humans are complex, and difficult.

In the early 2020s a series of record-busting temperatures worldwide began to register, pushing towards the high forties Celsius in British Columbia, Italy and Spain, and breaking 50 degrees in India, the Middle East and North Africa. Even Scotland, one of the most temperate countries in the world, registered heat of just under 35, too hot for the elderly and vulnerable to be outside in the direct sun.

'We're already past 1.5 degrees of warming', Jaime says matter-of-factly, pointing to the official stats that are about to be published when we speak. 'We're already seeing sea-level rise and coastal erosion across the UK; we're talking about places in India that are regularly getting up to fifty degrees now, where it isn't safe.'

There's a tension between the urgency of the climate crisis and the calm managerialism that has crept into politics. The campus recruitment stands for multinational consultancies emphasise the point, as do the funding calls for innovative fixes that drop into my inbox. Climate change is shoehorned into the language of everyday politics, as if it can simply be dealt with through competence and good intentions. In truth it is an existential question that transcends and eclipses all of our current understandings of how the world unfolds.

We are now seeing climate effects that many researchers had not anticipated until the 2050s. I have stood in a forest in the Swedish sub-arctic with temperatures over 30 degrees and the smell of dry pine needles rising from the dust of the forest floor, sat in Indian traffic jams in autumn heatwaves with the air so warm and moist that it is impossible to cool down naturally, and seen the Mediterranean coast burn. Whether we like it or not, we are already in the middle of something unprecedented.

I'm on research leave from work and in bed recovering from another relapse in a cheap flat in Marseilles when the email comes. Away from the pressure to teach classes and constantly monitor my inbox, my body has decided it wants only to rest. Late October in the south of France is like Scottish summer, and I can sit at the breakfast table with no shirt and a cup of coffee typing on my laptop until it is time to go out and work in the municipal library. Even by Mediterranean standards it is disconcertingly warm. On the laptop screen scenes unfold in real time of catastrophic flooding in

Valencia, eight hundred kilometres down the coast. It isn't exactly near but it is nearer than Scotland, only a train ride away.

Can you go? Usual fee, file by Wednesday? It's an editor for a magazine I write for now and then. I don't speak Spanish very well, but I message a few contacts – a Catalan colleague, a Glaswegian journalist and a Spanish TV reporter – asking for fixers. I'm in two minds about whether going is the right choice, but I feel like I should. I throw my camera and the microphone into the bag, reserve a seat on the next connection to Barcelona, and walk to the station.

I roll into Valencia in the early dark, moving at a crawl down the only railway into the city that has not been washed away. In the central station lines of empty trains sit without tracks to run on and the platforms are deserted. I am the only passenger in the carriage, and I find myself in an empty hotel lobby where lounge music plays on incongruously while the TV on the wall reports the rising death toll and broadcasts helicopter shots of what looks like the backdrop to a civil war.

When it gets light the following morning I find Carlos waiting for me outside the hotel as agreed. He's a local culture journalist who learned to speak English by listening to The Smiths and Joy Division as a teenager, reassigned by his editors in Madrid to cover the devastation. We've been hooked up by a mutual contact in Barcelona. We talk about Ian Curtis and The Jesus and Mary Chain on the walk to the edge of the old town and the bridges across the River Turia, past police checkpoints where the smell of stagnant water rises in the morning heat and Spanish army trucks buzz past carrying troops and bulldozers. The old town of Valencia is intact, but the suburbs across the river are unrecognisable.

We wade through the avenues with our cameras and microphone, recording the soundscape of rumbling truck engines and urgent voices, mud being turned on shovels like dough on a baker's table and the low hum of water pumps clearing basements to recover remains. Eventually we reach one of the stations of the Valencia Metro and I climb inside the shell of the ticket office for a closer look. The wall has been ripped away and the barriers to the platform are wrapped in trees that have rammed through the window and settled against the concrete floor. Wires from the signalling control cabinets have been ripped clear and burst from the rubble in colourful bundles of plastic. The overhead cables that power the trains are at ground level, shorted out and dangling precariously over the gulf where the tracks used to be. Carlos encourages me not to stay too long, pointing to a crack in the side of the room that runs down to the foundations.

Climate disaster takes many forms, but flooding is the quickest and most destructive. The Valencia flood happened after ocean warming had accelerated the evaporation rate and rain gathered in a pressure pocket, being blown inland until it hit the mountains and came down in a cloudburst that lasted all day. Water, 150 million cubic metres of it, surged down the narrow river gorges of the flood plain and through town after town, ripping up concrete bridges and pulling apartments into the torrent. Overnight, 30,000 people became homeless and 200 were dead, trapped in their cars or swept away where they stood on the exposed open ground.

We scramble up a bridge embankment over a drainage channel where the remains of a car lie crushed against the rocks, ripped apart by boulders carried on the current. Carlos whistles slowly as we round each new corner and the scale of the destruction becomes ever clearer. In the remains of one house the balloons for a child's birthday party are still strung from the rafters, the doors ripped off by the weight of the water. The floor of the building has disappeared. In many places the houses have simply folded into the river, concrete dust mixing with the silt as it pushed onwards, drawn by gravity and propelled by more water behind, a huge swirling kinetic bomb.

We walk for almost twenty kilometres in a loop through the flood-damaged towns and villages, everywhere caked in the same sediment torn from mountain valleys and orange groves and dumped on the coastal plain. The divers charged with retrieving bodies from still-flooded basements pull off their wetsuits in the autumn sun and churches hand out soup, clothing and bottled water to residents and volunteers. Everywhere are lives upended and ended.

Eventually we make it to an industrial estate on the southern fringe of the city. Carlos stands outside to make a call and I venture into the desolate underground car park of an IKEA store. In the half-light I start to feel dizzy. The adrenaline of the last twenty-four hours is beginning to fade, and everything takes on the unreal quality that falls over me whenever my brain starts to tire. The edges soften, and as my eyes adjust to the dark I can see the thick river mud where it has settled, flood water moulding it into regular patterns like tidal flats at low water. The motion sensors on the lights in the ceiling catch my movement and one by one they come on, stretching off to the far wall between the concrete pillars. In the distance the sign showing the way upstairs to the showroom flickers on and off, the name of the store illuminated in a cheery neon yellow. The posters promising unbelievable prices on furniture essentials in the familiar sans-serif font sit marooned above the mud-filled parking bays.

The setting sun eats the shadows on the walk back to the city up the remains of an intercity railway line. At a bar on the city fringe we are handed cold bottles of beer. We are part of a conveyor belt of clean-up volunteers, aid workers and the media at sunset heading back for showers and rest. I sit properly for the first time all day, dazed. The beer hits my stomach and just below it is another feeling, the guilt of being able to step away when the suffering carries on. I slink back to the hotel to file copy. As soon as I press 'send' I throw myself into the shower and watch the brown water take the dust off my cheeks and forearms, before falling into bed and sleeping for ten hours. When I wake the next day my boots are beyond repair, saturated with river mud and dirty water.

The following night I meet up for a drink with another Scottish journalist in Barcelona. She asks how it was and I say I'm fine, then pause and admit that I'm probably not.

One effect of brain trauma is hypersensitivity: the brain loses its ability to filter noise and you hear everything at equal volume. Conversations, car horns, children's screams and the screech of subway wheels all come through in high definition, to the point of being unbearable. If we could hear all the noise around us at its real volume it would be maddening, just as we would be driven to insanity if we could see all the events going on around the world in real time instead of dipping in and out, turning them off and getting up to make coffee or go to sleep in warm sheets on a quiet street.

Conflict and foreign journalists returning home often experience post-traumatic stress, as do climate correspondents who have seen the scale of disaster climate change can unleash first-hand. Not only are they exposed to destruction and human suffering, but when they return they struggle with the fact that other people seem uninterested in what they have to say, or refuse to take on board the consequences. If you stare at the world long enough it will stare back into you. Once you hear the noise you cannot easily unhear it.

I'm out of meds – left on the table in Marseilles in my rush to leave – and my head recycles scenes from the day before. I leave the bar and walk down the street to a line of people waiting outside the Sala Apolo, a club a few blocks back from the sea front. I want to drown my brain in noise, watching the floor of people murmurate from the balcony as the DJ works them, sinking cold glasses of Catalan beer and leaning into the wall. As the crowds spill onto the street and the clock pushes towards midnight I wander back to my bed up the El Paral·lel, with the distinct feeling of living outside time.

When I get home from France and Spain they have hung banners at the front of the university, banners celebrating the two-hundredth anniversary of Lord Kelvin's birth, while the river that became a metonym for scientific progress drops down through the park and towards the Clyde and the sea. The peregrines circle over the campus and the river gorge, out above the decommissioned coal docks and the footprints of shipyards and the statue of Lord Kelvin in Kelvingrove Park, soaring on the thermals. In the distance a rainstorm is brewing over the Firth of Clyde, ready to roll in and turn the grey pavements silver. We are all prisoners of thermodynamics, trapped under the same sky, trying to get out.

3

In a house, in a storm, at the end of the world

Shetland, late October. The plane dips through the clouds and there's a flash of cliffs and open water before the landing gear screeches against the wet tarmac of the airport runway, jutting into the North Sea at one end and the Atlantic at the other across a narrow spit of land.

I'm back for the first time in a while – Shetland is as far as you can get on a domestic flight in Scotland, or twelve hours overnight on the boat from Aberdeen. It's been six years, but Sumburgh Airport is the same as it was before the pandemic and before I got ill, and the same as it has been since the oil boom arrived. The 1970s terminal, built off the back of the discovery of North Sea petrocarbons, is ringed by small twin-engine turboprops and offshore helicopters resting at their stands, waiting for passengers. Every so often a new light appears in the mist and floats down towards the runway, the chop of the rotor engines growing louder before the whole helicopter becomes visible under the floodlights of the terminal.

I'd fled the university straight after class and jumped in a taxi to the airport to catch the small propeller plane with its tartan tailfin. Scotland is bound together by subsidised ferries and air routes, tiny aircraft and boats no bigger than large trawlers that go out in all weathers. Without them the outland of the Highlands and Islands simply could not exist.

I pick up the key that has been left for me at the rental counter and struggle in the wind to the car. Shetland is three hundred miles north of Glasgow and the light turns quickly, still two months out from the solstice. By the time I set off up the road towards my destination the murk has set in fully, white headlights bobbing behind and red tail lamps ahead. Everyone is heading for the warmth of home as the wind beats the sides of the cars and the short autumn tips over into long winter.

I'm going to a house in a side valley that falls from the hills of central Shetland to a sheltered inlet, halfway up the mainland, the long sliver of green in a grey sea that makes up the majority of the archipelago. The house is borrowed from a Shetlander journalist gone away to cover the war in Ukraine, south then south again to where Russian gas is pumped into Western Europe to keep people warm, paying for the bombs that are dropped on Ukrainian cities. Some of the refugees displaced by the occupation have done the reverse journey, taken in by Shetlanders until it is safe to return home.

It's a good house, the kind that have popped up all over Scotland in the past decade, built by people who can afford them. There's a German heat pump and thick glazing that means the inside is warm and airtight, wooden floors and large panoramic windows with views back down to the voe. Even so, the wind howls under the eaves and the rain machine-guns the windows from both directions.

When North Sea oil was discovered at the tail end of the 1960s, Shetland was in the right place at the right time. Many of the biggest oil fields were far out into the North

Atlantic and northern North Sea. The weather conditions meant that taking the product on and off rigs by boat was out of the question: the prize was too valuable. It would need to be piped and loaded in a safe port where large tankers could dock, an entire technological megasystem built from scratch in the coal-black waters of the North Sea winter. Local politicians realised this too, and lobbied heavily for a way to profit from the gold rush. The solution was a landing fee – for every barrel of oil that passed through the new Sullom Voe terminal on the north part of the Shetland mainland, Shetland would take a few crumbs. To the oil multinationals it was small change, but to the islanders it was transformative. A construction boom built a miniature welfare state off the back of the oil money, as well as creating jobs. Shetland found itself at the centre of international petrocapitalism, happily swimming in the wake of the energy giants wading into the North Atlantic.

People in the rest of Scotland talk about Shetland as a glimpse of what could have been. Shetlanders tripled their wages overnight, and workers from the declining industries of Glasgow and the Scottish coalfields came north to work as technicians, riggers and drivers. Their children grew up in a society moving upwards as the mainland slipped into slow decline. Even today Shetland is full of people in their fifties and sixties with Glasgow accents and stories to tell about getting on the boat north with nothing but a pair of work boots and a holdall.

The Shetland oil fund is worth £377 million, all sitting in a bank account managed by the members of the Shetland Islands Council. It sounds a lot, but since the 2008 financial crisis there has been less and less money available from London or Edinburgh and the oil fund has merely plugged the gap.

The UK is one of the largest economies in the world, but it does not always feel like it. Scotland is also one of the few regions outside the south-east of England that more than pays for itself, due to oil and now renewable energy, tourism, whisky and education. In 2014, when Scotland came close to voting for independence, a huge part of the attraction was the prospect of using some of that wealth to flee the constant cutbacks and dominance of London, as schools and hospitals crumbled and libraries cut their opening hours or disappeared completely. People have seen the welfare state drip away quicker than oil dribbles in, and even in Shetland poverty is back and the struggles of everyday life in the UK are evident; food banks and unpayable heating bills, people struggling to finance mortgages, and a feeling that even here – at the heart of the oil economy – something has gone badly wrong.

As oil declined and public spending was slashed, Shetland started to think about what it could do to stem the losses. There was supposed to be a public stake in a new wind project called Viking that generates millions of pounds a year, but the private company that built it ended up as the sole owner, due to disagreements locally and a lack of support from the national government. Whereas the oil fund brought wealth for all, Shetland has ended up being shut out of what was sold as the solution to the end of the oil boom. Shetlanders now see huge wind turbines every day on their drive down the spine of the archipelago, making money for someone else as the society around them starts to show the cracks of long-term neglect. It's one of the reasons I've come back, a place where the ironies of the energy economy are writ large.

The weather is still going strong, with driving rain and wind, as I travel the same road back south the following morning to do an interview. Viking dominates central Shetland day and night. The turbines are 150m high, feeding floodlit transformer stations that connect to undersea cables back to the rest of the world. The towers have red marker lights that blink in the black over the rooftops of the croft houses.

I've agreed to meet Tom, a renewables consultant who works from an office up the hill from the harbour in Lerwick, and who was one of the loudest voices in Shetland for Scottish independence. He texts me and says he's staying at home because of family commitments and the weather, but that I can come over for lunch if I like and he'll do right by me with some soup for my troubles. By come over he means on the boat, a ten-minute ride across the harbour to Bressay, the long, low island that faces the Lerwick docks and makes the town a natural refuge from the easterly gales that blow in.

The boat leaks the fuggy warmth of electric bar heaters that numb the hands and leave my brain in a gentle haze, slowly burning the dust on the seat coverings to give the passenger cabin the scent of charred newspaper mixed with saltspray and rust. She has room for twenty cars and a broken vending machine against one wall. I am the only passenger. This boat is a relic of a time when there was money for big projects, and she rumbles across the sound, day after day until money can be found to relieve her. I look at the builder's plate – she's almost as old as me, built in Glasgow at the back end of the eighties, when the city still had the capacity to turn out tugs, ferries and freighters.

Tom meets me at the other end. He throws my kit into the back of his 4x4 and we head off down the single road that winds from Bressay pier to the houses along the island's lee side. We pull up at a property restored piece by piece by Tom's parents, a custom construction made and remade as resources allow with ad hoc lean-tos and a cottage garden around the skeleton of the old croft house. Tom's dad, Jonathan, is a legendary figure in Shetland life, a local public intellectual born of the do-it-yourself ethic of 1960s political counter-culture and unafraid to turn his hand to whatever needs dealing with. He's now in his retirement, and an office full of papers and a lifetime of books in one of the extensions sit waiting for their owner to return from the mainland.

Tom fixes us a salad from the garden – raised beds protected from the wind and small greenhouses that mean the house can feed itself. The weather can be heavy in Shetland but it never gets that cold. The Gulf Stream brings warmer water up from the central Atlantic in a conveyor motion, though scientists are worried it could be on the verge of collapse. Like the coast of Norway to the east and Faroe to the north-west, the sea stops the mercury rising too high or going below freezing. It isn't the best place to farm, but nor is it the worst. The Vikings happily colonised Shetland as part of their Atlantic kingdom. The all-time high temperature record is a liveable 27 degrees, a strong Norwegian summer day.

Tom is not much older than the ferry either, born at the same time as me and gone away and come home again, to South America and Glasgow and back to Bressay. The accent is still there, a soft Shetland burr that doesn't sound all that Scottish to people weaned on TV portrayals of hard-man Glaswegians and Edinburgh socialites. He's the same height as me too, towering out of his wellies as he pulls the lettuce from the ground.

The drum of the rain on the roof of the lean-to dining room is so loud it drowns out the microphone and we have to stop recording. Tom's voice vanishes completely against the hammer of the droplets slamming in from the east. He beckons me into the living room under the tiled roof, where pictures of the family frame the windows with their view out over the sound and back to Lerwick. I check the levels and he is coming through fine, so we start again.

Tom was involved in installing a set of tidal turbines in the narrow sound up between the islands of Unst and Yell at the very top of Shetland, one of the first big deployments once the technology started to mature. He now works for a consultancy called Voar – a North Isles word meaning spring – that is locally owned and is arguing for more than crumbs from the table of the renewables revolution. Often when a big project comes along, locals get to make the sandwiches and not much more, as Tom puts it.

'I'm keen to see that benefits the taxpayer and the community more than it has in the past', he says.

I ask him about the Viking wind farm and he is forthright about the fallout.

'It's a live question – I think it's a tragedy the forty-five per cent community stake was lost', he tells me, pointing out that one mega-project will bring Shetland less each year than a small community-run wind farm in a field further up the archipelago.

Viking has reminded Shetlanders that energy companies bearing gifts are not always a good thing. It is the biggest single engineering project in Shetland since the massive Sullom Voe terminal was built in the 1970s, and there is more to follow as offshore wind comes online. On the face of it, it puts Shetland on the renewables map, a green energy destination in a world crying out for carbon-free power. Waiting for the flight up I'd watched a video made a few months before by an American news channel about how oil-loving Shetland was moving into a new chapter. It completely failed to mention that none of the profits were going into the public purse, in Shetland or in Scotland as a whole.

Even with climate change and visible decline, people are still broadly positive about oil in Shetland. Tom makes the point that it is easy to stay loyal to the fossil industry when it creates good jobs at home and the worst impacts of atmospheric warming are still very far away. Climate change is there in Shetland if you know where to look, but the wool shops of central Lerwick still do a good trade in jumpers for visitors piling off the cruise ships unprepared. Shetland is beautiful, but it is not always pleasant.

We finish the interview and I wrap up the microphone and headphones and put them back in my rucksack.

'If you're around on Saturday you should come back. Dad'll be here', Tom says as he drives me to the boat. 'You can do the run.'

The next time I see Tom he's in a cook's apron behind the counter of the café in Bressay's community hall, producing bacon rolls to order on a gas stove. The island holds a 5km race every Saturday and people come in from all over the archipelago to take part, finishing in the hall, where they are invited to mainline carbohydrates and caffeine to recover. It boosts spending in the small community and raises money for the island. There are always a few interlopers like me, fresh off the boat or up for work.

Before the accident I used to run a lot and play as a defensive midfielder for a couple of different football teams, covering six or seven kilometres in the space of ninety minutes if I was doing my job properly. Afterwards I could barely walk in a straight line. COVID-19 caused one of my lungs to stop responding completely, and nobody could explain quite why. The doctors have me on a stepped recovery programme, and I'm not sure 5km in the Shetland wind is a good idea, but Tom assures me that the finish line is the

place to get all of Shetland in one place and an opportunity
to get to know islanders. A picture of me looking like death
as I round the final corner is posted on the community social
media page, giving a weak thumbs-up that fools nobody.
The race is won by a lean Australian of indeterminate age
who works at one of the local fish farms. He's already tucking
into his brunch by the time I pull myself through the café
door.

When the dishes are done Tom swings by to pick up some
washing from his place down the lane and we head back
along the bay to the family home. Tom's dad is here, playing
in the office with his grandchildren, the computer blinking
away behind him as he edits new writing.

Jonathan is an older iteration of the man from the family
photos in the lounge, the same broad smile and thick beard
greyed by his seventies. The latest book in his extensive
corpus draws on seemingly endless material from a life well
lived. He wrote one of the first accounts of big oil in Shetland,
stood for the Labour Party in the British Parliament, became
a councillor in Shetland and served as editor of the local
newspaper and boatman to the Muckle Flugga lighthouse
at the northernmost extremity of the archipelago. When we
find him, he's sorting through photos from travelling in
pre-liberalisation China, digitised and slightly over-exposed
pictures of happy explorers posing in empty squares and
vignettes of a society about to be transformed.

'Shetland has never been a backwater. The metropolitan
chauvinist idea is that it's far away and remote, and it isn't
– it's at a crossroads in the North Sea', says Jonathan when
I ask him about Shetland's transformation at the hands of
the oil industry. It was coal, not oil, that first industrialised
Shetland when steam-powered trawlers began the age of
deep-water fishing, and then two wars fought in the North

Atlantic made Shetland and Orkney into naval strongholds and brought money and technology.

At its peak Shetland was home to thirty thousand people, but by the time oil arrived in the late 1960s it was down to little more than half of that. Jonathan was young when the oil came, but there were older heads who refused to just roll over.

'Shetland knew about oil because Shetland men had been sailing on oil tankers for a hundred years. They knew the mess that had been made in Venezuela, they knew the mess in the Niger Delta the oil industry had made. They were determined it wouldn't happen here', he says, leaning in knowingly. 'The problem is, somebody forgot that there are seven point four barrels of oil in a tonne, and they got a royalty of twopence per tonne instead of per barrel.'

In the early 1970s Britain was dealing with decolonisation and deindustrialisation, stagnant growth after twenty years of post-war reconstruction, and an existential crisis about its place in the world. The global oil crisis of 1973 had far-reaching impacts, and the UK government was in desperate need of income. North Sea revenues were the only kind of money around, and Shetland was suddenly much more than a romantic outpost that sent one MP to the parliament seven hundred miles away.

The oil industry is a catch-all term for everything from cigar-smoking directors in Texan boardrooms to the people who clean the toilets on the rigs. Not all oil jobs are equal, especially in the fossil economy. As revenues have declined and profit margins narrowed, a new breed of asset managers have started to carve up and exploit what remains of the North Sea oil boom.

'The new bunch who've taken over now are basically venture capitalists, they don't know much about oil', says

Jonathan, with a hint of nostalgia for the age of the big British and American companies. The vultures are picking up the most valuable assets and squeezing them dry. Workers suddenly find themselves with new paymasters, or hived off to service companies as the industry atomises. Sullom Voe is now run by a group called EnQuest, not an oil company as much as an investment vehicle to pull together the profitable bits of the North Sea and extract what shareholder value it can.

Viking may be zero-carbon, but the ownership is not all that different from the rigs and oil terminals around the Shetland coast, run by one large renewables company which in turn is owned by international banks and hedge funds. On the list of beneficiaries is an American investment fund that also has significant portfolios in weapons manufacturing and has been subject to protests for the profits it has made from the bombing of the Gaza Strip. Shetland is a long way from the Middle East, but the investors who grew rich from weapons and oil have no qualms about renewables if it keeps the stock price stable.

When the Bressay shuttle touches the dock in Lerwick again the south boat – the ferry to Aberdeen and the mainland – is in and a rainbow has built a temporary bridge across the sound. You needn't spend much time in the North Atlantic to understand why the rainbow was central to Norse mythology, appearing out of the half-rain in low sun as the weather rolls in and out.

I've a friend who used to work as a housing officer for the council in Lerwick, not far off the harbour. He told me how people with clipped English accents and dreams of a new start, propelled by questionable ideas about the utopian potential of Shetland, would arrive fresh off the ferry and come to his office asking to be given somewhere to live.

The North had called them, they would invariably say, and they expected him to facilitate their quests. It is Shetland's bad luck that along with Alaska and the Canadian interior it is the most northerly English-speaking place on earth. People quit jobs in banks and marketing companies, media empires and hedge funds to come and find a simpler way of life. A retired GP who had done a ten-year stint in Shetland told me how people would come to the practice in Lerwick with depression or domestic problems as their dreams of island life shattered against the immovable rock wall of reality, pitching up in the waiting room with failed marriages and businesses or seasonal affective disorder. Shetland is as subject to the contradictions and burdens of everyday life as anywhere else.

Unst and Yell are different from the rest of Shetland. There are even fewer trees, and noticeably fewer people. Back before the oil, before the new double-track roads and the diesel ferries with their coffee machines and reinforced bows, there was a passenger steamer that did a circuit out from Lerwick and back again a few times a week, bringing people and post. The military have a base up here too, a radar station at Saxa Vord in Unst, built to look out for Soviet bombers and intercontinental ballistic missiles destined for English cities. If you draw a missile trajectory from the Russian interior to England it passes right over Shetland. Nobody ever thought the Russian threat would one day come back.

The North Isles were where Jonathan moved to in the 1970s as a returning student, pushing against the current to farm on the more remote crofts and create a little alternative society on the outermost islands with dreams of a Shetland renaissance. On the mainland, meanwhile, migrant workers flooded into temporary camps to build the Sullom Voe terminal, a military operation bigger than anything NATO could muster that created a city of wooden huts and mess halls on the hill above the Yell ferry terminal.

I leave the car at the pier and take my place in the passenger lounge. I'm the only occupant, trundling across the water to Yell on a growing swell. I've been given instructions by someone speaking through a bad line from the top of Unst, but I think I'm in the right place. Waiting for me is a woman called Alice, who works for the local development company, wearing the standard-issue outdoor jacket and jeans, the winter uniform of most people in Shetland. She's a Shetlander by choice rather than birth, but in the islands English and international accents are not the cultural shibboleths they become in the Central Belt. It takes all sorts to build a community, or in the case of Unst and Yell, to rebuild it.

The wind is growing unpleasantly cold and the skies are beginning to darken. I'd wanted to go out on the boat to see the tidal turbines, but it was too dangerous, so instead I was invited up to see the community wind farm before the weather came in. It's the same one Tom had told me about a few days before. The two ferries, *Daggri* and *Dagalien*, named after the Norse words for dawn and dusk, ply the channel in unison and cross in the middle of the sound day and night. Alice drives as we burn up the fast oil road to the northern half of the island. From there another ferry goes to Unst, but she's tied up firmly at the dock and probably won't run again as long as the wind keeps up. The Shetlanders look enviously to Norway, where the oil money has paid for undersea tunnels and bridges that are safer from the weather, and where unbelievable amounts of money have been poured into rural communities. In the 1950s western Norway was just like Shetland, relying on fishing and subsistence farming. Today it vies annually with Switzerland for first place in the human development index, while Scotland has a creaking infrastructure and a child poverty rate of 24 per cent.

We pull up outside a low concrete hall, the headquarters of the development company in an old business centre and garage. The islands of Scotland are littered with the leftovers of various public and private investments that never quite fulfilled their promise, some abandoned and some repurposed. In a side room the remains of a loom sit waiting to be collected, a relic of a drive to support weaving the fine wool for which Shetland is known. The whole place is still wet with industrial paint and the heating is off. What warmth there was has leached into the concrete. This is one of the few places in Britain that is genuinely remote – either you do things here yourself or they don't get done.

Another car pulls up and out gets Andrew, the head of the development company. He exchanges a few words with Alice and I repeat the details again. It's a hastily arranged trip and she fills him in on who I am and what I want. I mouth some familiar lines – I'm glad they've taken the time to see me after coming this far. Alice says goodbye and leaves, desperate to get home and into a heated sitting room.

In his seventies, Andrew speaks with the thicker dialect of an older generation. He's from Yell, and he's come back to Yell. He's been at sea, worked at the oil terminal, and is now one of the driving figures in the campaign to bring the island back from a precipice. The community company has three turbines they built themselves that give them power – both literally and figuratively – providing the islanders with some kind of sovereignty in a world where energy is currency. He beckons me into a tiny kitchen, the one warmish room in the hall, and we perch on flimsy folding chairs. The microphone recordings echo off the bare concrete and the wind is audibly picking up outside as the sound bars jump through yellow and into the red on the monitor.

Yell's energy independence was built out of necessity. The island is not a hugely profitable place to build corporate windmills for corporate windfalls, but the islanders went ahead anyway, and they did it without big government grants. The project took fifteen years, and unlike the multinational mega projects, there were no teams of lawyers to push it through.

The red gusts on the microphone make me think about heading back to the mainland before the weather takes, but Andrew wants to show me the turbines. We power across cattle grids and through locked gates before coming to a halt on the gravel at the top of the hill overlooking North Yell, the blades beating double time in the early dusk. He opens up the door at the base of one of them and we climb the steps through the metal oval. Inside it looks like the electrical room of a diesel-turbine boat. Andrew shows me the live outputs, the wind speeds and the transformers. It's easy to see how seamanship and crofting transfers to the wind economy. Andrew is like a farmer showing off his prize rams, or cash cows.

'We'd seen what happened on other Scottish islands, in Gigha and in Orkney in particular', Andrew says under the thrum of the blades. 'The community wind farm does about eight to ten per cent of Shetland's electricity; before that it would have been diesel.'

Although Shetland is a major oil producer, the further you get from urban centres the more you have to pay for energy. One of the ironies of fossil fuels is that huge amounts are used just to ferry it about. Electricity, on the other hand, will go anywhere you lead it; you just have to provide a path of least resistance. Anything that reduces the reliance of places far from hubs of power and energy is welcome, climate change or not.

The storm keeps growing and there's a visible chop on the sound down by the Unst ferry. Beyond that the open sea spreads itself menacingly northwards towards the Arctic Circle. Across the sound the domes of the Saxa Vord radar brace for the impact, exposed on the hilltop to the boreal winds. The development company is also investing in climate resilience hubs at local halls, where people can go and cook, sleep and keep warm in extreme weather events if the power goes out or their homes flood. Even here, far from the forest fires and floods, the climate crisis is leaking into the frame among the cold blues and blacks of the rolling sea.

The storm wind whistles ever stronger in the wires of the ship's flag as the *Daggri* bumps into the pier of mainland terminal, her stern swinging around to inch up to the jetty in the swell. The car is there waiting for me, rocking on its suspension, and I drive to the café in Brae on the other side of the hill, past Sullom Voe and the burning tower of the gas terminal run by Total, the French energy giant.

EnQuest are not interested in letting me inside – despite some impressive animations on video screens at the airport and press releases, the future is not quite ready for viewing, or rather, I'm not of use to them. For years energy companies made sizeable donations to Scotland's universities in the name of science, but they don't like it when they don't get something back.

By 1993 Sullom Voe had pumped six billion barrels of liquid assets; by 2010 it was eight billion, as production slowed but stayed steady. If all that oil were sold today it would have a market value in the hundreds of billions of dollars. When I try to find out exactly how much the oil and gas coming through Sullom Voe has been worth to the oil companies it's almost impossible. It suits them to stay vague on just how little Shetland has. Jonathan estimated it as being just a few weeks' worth of production over the decades the terminal has run.

As I sit in the car park a man appears carrying a small boy. It's Karl, a face from a past life when I worked in another university sociology department on a different coast. His son hides behind his legs, shy of the stranger with the rucksack and microphone he can't remember meeting before. A lot of your thirties is about watching your friends become their parents, having your eyes opened to the realities of a stage of life you had only ever observed second-hand, through snatched conversations around door frames and from the back seat of a car. The sensation is something like learned empathy, tempered by the baggage of upbringing.

It's just luck that we're in Shetland at the same time – Karl is back here to show his son the villages he grew up in and to escape the demands of a university system suffering under the effects of cutbacks and micromanagement. He's happier out here with his family and his field than in the anxiety machine of grant applications, overwork and academic hustle.

Karl grew up in Brae but was born up in Yell, and his mum worked the oil camps as a cleaner. One of his pet projects has been tracing the work of Erving Goffman, the pioneer of human behavioural analysis who carried out his early fieldwork at Baltasound in Unst. The result, *The Presentation of the Self in Everyday Life*, became one of the landmark texts of twentieth-century American sociology. Living at the top of Shetland, not far from Saxa Vord, Goffman used it as a laboratory to understand how people act out public and private roles, laying the foundations for a whole sub-field of social science focused on life as drama. As I drive around with my microphone I slip into the role of the academic and the people I speak to act out the answers they think I probably want. It's a hard mode to break out of.

Goffman spent enough time in Unst to grasp how difficult life could be in the Northern Isles, at a time when there were no helicopter evacuations or internet, no heated resilience hubs and no oil roads. In 1950, when Goffman was here, the systems of self-sufficiency and community co-dependence that had characterised island communities for hundreds of years were still more or less intact.

Karl was born into the new Shetland, a world of high petro-capitalism, where the Sullom Voe terminal was still pumping millions of barrels of oil a year and the tax receipts were feeding into Shetland's bank account and the UK Treasury in London. Each time he comes back he sees the slow decline of the oil: the closed restaurant that used to cater to oil workers, the swimming pool that has cut its hours. The local helicopter terminal at Scatsta, east of Brae, closed five years before and the whole site is now a ghost town, grass beginning to take back the runway and empty hangars and baggage conveyors awaiting phantom bags.

'Almost every other home would have somebody who was either at Sullom Voe and Scatsta. We all knew the flight timetables and which helicopters were which', he says as he chews on his Shetland haddock. 'It's what made Brae exist and continue to exist.'

'There's kids I went to school with who came up with the apprenticeships and those are going, the helicopters are going and a lot of engineering work is going. It feels like a slow winding down.'

I mention the wind farm and he pauses to make sure his answer is nuanced enough.

'Viking? It would have allowed us to do things economically that we can't do now.'

He sees the future with the clear eyes of the returnee, torn between a love of the place and the bigger opportunities of the cities. In his late teens he worked in a factory producing polystyrene packaging for frozen fish to be sent to London, North Sea fish and North Sea plastics in the ultimate Shetland hamper. Industrial fishing and industrial oil production have both been good for the islands, but their success has bred indifference too. Shetland should be an in insurmountable position as a green powerhouse, but instead it is the polluting diesel ferries to the mainland that keep the islanders supplied and the oil and the fish that goes out in exchange.

As if to make the point, Radio Shetland reports that the boats are off, with the storm forecasts looking severe. Karl makes a move for home and we pull on our jackets and head to the car park. As I leave he stops me – 'I know you know this but make sure you've got stuff in, because the shops will be empty for a few days.'

I dutifully stock up on cans and bread, as everyone else does too. The supermarket shelves empty in an afternoon. Storm Babet – the second big one of the season – hits fully that night, mercifully calmer than further south, where it takes lives and hauls down power lines. The Lerwick lifeboat is out for eighteen hours rescuing a trawler sixty miles offshore, flung about in three dimensions at once without power and drifting uncontrollably.

As the last light falls away to the south I drive the loop road down the eastern side of the Shetland mainland with the wipers on full, watching the swell break onto the reefs in the headlights. The trawlermen coming into Bressay Sound for shelter report seven-metre waves near to shore and worse further out, inching towards the top of the sea-state scale.

I push on home in the dark, where I drift in and out of light sleep as the wind comes at the house from all directions and the orange and blue flashes of emergency vehicles light up the curve of the main road across the voe.

When I wake up the next day I find a tree-shaped dent in the car bumper. I must have hit something in the wind that had skipped across the coast road. I get an email from the airline; in Aberdeen one of the planes on the tarmac has been damaged by the storm and my flight back to mainland Scotland is cancelled too. Lerwick port is a gallery of oil boats, deep-sea fishing vessels and the ferries confined to their quay that should be carrying food and tourists, locked into port by the weather.

It turns out the emergency lights were for one of the cars that had thundered down the hill an hour before. The road up to Sullom Voe is closed after a head-on collision in the dark, one car crunching into another at a combined speed of 120 mph, coming around a bend in the road, thousands of tiny explosions moving the metal boxes towards each other at the speed of oil. There's one hospital in Shetland and it's a long way away at midnight in winter. Both drivers survived, I find out afterwards, but the cars were write-offs.

Eventually the storm subsides, four days after it first drifted in, and for a few hours the sky over the Atlantic turns blue again, golden threads of sun casting themselves onto the west mainland. The narrow firths and fields of Shetland's Westside glow in the afternoon heat as I take the long way back south to the airport, stopping to watch seals basking in the clear weather. When the clock hits five the sun starts to fall onto the invisible mainland beyond the southern horizon and I turn onto the airport perimeter road with a line of helicopters coming in from the rigs, extra flights to catch up after three days of being grounded. Men delayed on their way home sit in the lounge sinking bottles of lager until the flight to Edinburgh is called. In front of us, a charter paid for by the oil companies carries a single passenger and some supplies to Aberdeen.

Our plane is given the all-clear by the control tower and arcs into the evening and back towards Orkney, Caithness and the hills of the Eastern Highlands. Under us the gas flares of the North Sea flicker, mapping out the mosaic of extraction points in the sea floor as the carbon rises into the atmosphere and mingles with the exhaust gases from the turboprop. The fuselage shakes, negotiating little changes in the density of the air, falling and rising as vapour maps out the eddies and peels off into a trail under the blinking wing lights.

4

A city of thorns

It's Friday, mid-evening, and central Glasgow is balanced between tides of people. Empty shopping streets and darkened office blocks are interrupted by the post-work crowd stumbling home from pubs, swapping glances with people in for a big night from the suburbs and the Lanarkshire satellite towns under the departure boards of Central Station.

The rain lashes in off the river, visible in the glow of the station clock. In Glasgow it doesn't so much rain or shine as fluctuate through stages of water. Humidity is often above 70 per cent for weeks, and when the air gets too heavy it breaks and turns to rain, then mist, then rain again. The air can be so moist that when the mercury falls below zero, in minutes the frost forms on the ground as thick as snow. The drum on the grand glass roof of the station, suspended from girders cast a few miles away in Motherwell furnaces burning with Lanarkshire coal, is the soundtrack to a Clyde winter.

From November to the end of February in Glasgow the darkness and the weather settle over the psyche and the body pushes back, craving light and movement. Some people simply cannot handle it, slipping into a malaise that lasts until spring. The airport is always busy with budget flights to places a thousand miles south, helping people escape Glasgow for temporary relief in Greece, Turkey and Portugal.

I never expected to end up back here – my parents had left their jobs in Glasgow and moved south before I was born, but it was always there in fragments. My earliest memories of the city are of trips to the fading museums with their stuffed animals and old buses, ice-skating at a 1980s shopping centre built on the rubble of an abandoned railway terminus, and staring through wire fences at lines of decommissioned diesel engines left to rot amongst the weeds.

I'm just old enough to have experienced the tail end of Glasgow's worst years, when the Clyde valley was reduced from one of the most important industrial centres in the world to a ghost city on the European fringe. When the French film director Bernard Tavernier wanted a location to film his adaptation of the dystopian science fiction novel *The Unsleeping Eye* he scouted Europe for somewhere that could do justice to the ambience of the novel before settling on Glasgow's blackened streets and empty city blocks. The resulting film, *Death Watch*, does for Glasgow what Wim Wenders did for Berlin, letting the camera roam across the ruins of a city that for a brief flash was at the centre of everything. It's what German romantics called *Ruinenlust*, the pleasure of ruin.

Tavernier follows his actors as they amble across half-demolished city blocks and down blackened avenues with the camera lurking behind, local children stumbling into shot and the very real desolation of abandoned dockyards and burned-out factories better than any set Hollywood could build. In one of the scenes a kid playing on a gravel park surrounded by broken railings runs up to Harvey Keitel and audibly shouts, 'Hey, mister, can I be in your picture?' in a thick Glasgow accent. Tavernier left it in, seemingly happy to accidentally break the fourth wall and let the audience see that the sets and extras were all real and organic. If you wanted a vision of the end of the developed world, then late 1970s Glasgow was the perfect canvas.

Keitel plays an ambitious TV cameraman who stalks the streets of the pollution-blackened city and its empty tenements in pursuit of Romy Schneider's supposedly terminally ill and unwilling reality-TV star. Behind the story something catastrophic but unnameable has happened; the characters make subtle references to inflation and food rationing without ever confronting whatever is behind the curtain. Keitel is a hustler looking for a big payday as the world crumbles around him, Schneider a cynical pulp-romance author who writes demographically targeted books with the aid of AI. Reality TV and computer-generated stories distract people from the horror of whatever is unseen yet omnipresent, and the only escape is to flee the city entirely. Tavernier understood that we have a spectacular collective capacity for denial and distraction, and that the end of the world is no exception.

Before its fall Glasgow was one of the most densely populated cities in Europe, more than a million people living where they worked and working where they lived over an area the same size as central London. After the Second World War the city lost half its population, some in the name of social improvement and new towns built as part of an expanding welfare state, but most of it due to almost total industrial and economic collapse. By the early 2000s there were fewer than sixty thousand people in the confines of old Glasgow. In 1945 there had been 1.2 million.

Glasgow become an involuntary laboratory for the effects of late capitalist deindustrialisation, accelerated by government policies of managed decline of its core industries.

Oxbridge-educated civil servants were dispatched from London to sell off and wind up what remained of the shipbuilding industry, the same people who would be sent to the Soviet Union after the fall of the Berlin Wall to help it adjust to the brave new world of the market.

My colleagues in the Sociology department at the university have spent decades mapping, querying and unpacking the multitude of factors that led to this spectacular transformation and its aftershocks. It has a name – the Glasgow Effect – a peculiar confluence of factors that made modern Glasgow poorer, sicker and largely forgotten. 'Nobody cares about Glasgow, so you can get away with a lot', as one of them put it. For better or worse, it holds up.

I live in an apartment created from one floor of a Victorian mansion that was abandoned in the 1950s and then subdivided into individual rooms with locks on the doors and gas stoves in the corner of each, catering to itinerant workers and university students. Under the cheap paint the last absentee landlord applied, the walls are still stained with the cigarette smoke of long 1960s evenings spent reading on camp beds by a bar fire.

In the 1990s property was so cheap that people would buy up whole houses or old warehouses and use them as ateliers and studios. For a brief moment the city threatened to become a Barcelona of the north, a grimy and dysfunctional but exciting place. Glasgow was, to steal a phrase from Berlin, poor but sexy.

Unlike Berlin though, where state money and international capital flooded in after reunification, Glasgow never fully recovered, economically and culturally. I sometimes think back to being a trainee journalist in Berlin in the early 2000s, living off nothing in apartments with mattresses on the floor and sofas made from shipping crates. We survived on cheap breakfasts from the local Turkish *Imbiss*, tap water and cheap beer. It didn't matter because we were surrounded by life, and we all had 'European Union' embossed on the front of our passports. That meant more to us than our home towns or first languages, and Berlin belonged to us as Europeans. We lived in a world that seemed to at least be heading in the right direction, even if things were far from perfect.

For one of my first independent reporting gigs my editor asked me to go to hear a speech by an American senator called Barack Obama, who had just announced his intention to run for the US presidency. He was pledging to tackle climate change, reform American foreign policy and pull people out of grinding working poverty with health care and education. I wove through the crowd doing vox pops with young Germans and American voters alike full of hope, funnelling it back to front pages in America. I think I believed in the words I committed to print.

A decade and a half is around one-fifth of an average human life, and a human lifespan is imperceptible in the history of the earth's climate, or at least used to be. In the fifteen years since Berlin and Obama's grand promises to cheering crowds, climate change has accelerated rapidly and is getting worse.

Standing on the railway station, under the hammering rain on the roof, I'm not long back again from a research visit to Kolkata, where the cities boil in humid heat and the wet-bulb temperature – the temperature shown by a thermometer wrapped in a wet cloth – has hit a dangerous threshold. Humans can survive in very hot conditions, but only if they can get the excess heat away fast enough. In a wet-bulb temperature above 32 degrees the body begins to experience severe heat stress and eventually systematic failure. The brain, liver and kidneys all reach the threshold of endurance. Enzymes crucial to bodily function break down and the brain overheats like a computer with a broken fan. The symptoms of heatstroke are remarkably similar to concussion and it can cause permanent brain damage.

A friend I work with based in California sends me regular updates on the spread of forest fires around San Francisco Bay and the heat warnings in place. She says she has fallen asleep dreaming of Glasgow's damp streets and the speckled rain of an Atlantic summer, her air conditioning knocked out by rolling blackouts to stop the power lines overheating because the energy companies haven't invested in the grid. Her brother is a firefighter who spends his summers being redeployed around the state to tackle wildfires with dwindling resources.

In Bertrand Tavernier's Glasgow the unnamed catastrophe lurking in the background has created an underclass of refugees, clustered in churches and alleyways or scraping a living at junk markets in the ruins of the abandoned docks. The real Glasgow already has its own refugees too, some living half-lives in cramped temporary rooms, some relegated to condemned housing schemes where nobody else lives or would want to. They've ended up here due to war, genocide, homophobia and political repression, but climate change will put more people on the move than ever before in human history. Cities with relatively liveable climates and space for development like Glasgow or Auckland will be prime destinations. Nowhere is safe from climate change, but some places are safer than others. Spain, India and California leave me grateful that this is my home, a place of relative calm.

Modern Glasgow is two cities linked by the cultural memory of when they were one, cut in half by an elevated motorway that sweeps through the southern suburbs and up over the Clyde before carving a swathe through the north side of town. As you drive through the city centre the metal roofs of warehouses and industrial units merge into car showrooms and patches of waste ground, the tell-tale signs of badly conceived urban renewal built on the rubble of communities that were cleared wholesale in the 1960s. When the motorway was built, a strip one hundred metres wide was ploughed through homes, public squares, hotels and shops. Students from the nearby art school hung a banner from the overbridges that simply read 'This is a scar that will never heal'.

The two halves of the city are joined by a few remaining roads and Glasgow's Subway, a miniature copy of the London Underground built during the city's industrial ascendancy but never expanded beyond a solitary line that rattles beneath the streets around underground streams and old mineshafts. It runs in a circle that takes less than half an hour to complete, passing the university before looping south to the former docks and back into the city again. Glasgow students do a pub crawl where they have to have a drink at each of the fifteen stations, barely standing by the time they complete the circuit. If you miss your train you merely get on the first one going in the other direction.

One of the least loved stops on the loop is St George's Cross, a narrow platform in a low tunnel between the running lines where it feels as if any misstep will send you tumbling into the path of a train. The damp of the tunnels is everywhere; the ceiling drips with condensation that forms a sheen on the wall tiles when the humidity rises. The station exit doesn't offer much respite from the sense of being pinned between walls, kicking you out into the underbelly of the motorway and its tendrils, robbed of any natural reference points.

This was once a busy junction where the major streets of the west side of Glasgow met, packed at rush hour with crowds of people dodging trams and ducking into department stores or heading through stairwell doors into apartments. The city tram network was massacred in the early 1960s, just as Glasgow's infamous ring of motorways began to become a reality. The new contours of the city were drawn seemingly arbitrarily by planners, a form of urban warfare in which whole futures were wiped out with the sweep of a hand across a table.

I emerge from the Subway station into the maze of traffic and crash barriers that passes for public space immediately outside. I rarely come to this corner of Glasgow, a no man's land between worlds where the rumble of car wheels is constant. It begins to rain again, running over the tarmac and leaching into the concrete in search of the water table and the river. I'm late, and dizzy with a headache that has started to numb the right side of my face. I think about calling off the interview but I've already cancelled once due to poor health and the sensation of time slipping away is more acute than usual. It doesn't help that the area around the road is a sensory torture chamber.

The place I'm looking for is one of the only old buildings left, a former printworks from the 1920s that lay derelict in the shadow of the concrete viaducts before being given a new life as an arts venue and office for artists and designers.

The canteen at the co-working space is packed with people on long benches, speaking to invisible colleagues on laptop screens sitting in East London, Brooklyn and Berlin. They're all part of the semiotic of contemporary innovation culture in which people are expected to look extremely relaxed and pathologically busy at the same time.

Scott gazes around the crowd before spotting me propped against the back wall, trying to sit up and organise my thoughts. There are two drinks waiting together with the microphone on the table, next to the dead batteries I have just pulled out of the recorder.

He is in his late twenties, with a ponytail, beard and lumberjack shirt to unintentionally match the general aesthetic. The food is vegan, the wood real rather than plastic veneer, and the building won a design award for its low-carbon credentials. He suggested meeting here: his office, but also an example of what he's trying to achieve.

'We could have been doing so much better for a long time', he says mournfully. Glasgow is a place of perpetual dreams and repeated missed opportunity. When Scott graduated from his university architecture degree at the end of the 2010s he had hoped to find work driven by sustainability and the climate crisis, expecting to find older and more experienced people who could take him on and teach him, but instead he ended up going solo and founding his own architectural consultancy, the Anthropocene Architecture School. The school is less a job than a vocation – radical architecture doesn't make anyone rich, and in Glasgow the money is in mass value-engineered projects of identikit homes and supposedly luxury developments with floor space smaller than a 1960s council house.

The children of the late 1990s and early 2000s came of age in an era of climate optimism that has slowly turned to exasperation. Scotland only had its parliament restored in 1999, after a three-hundred-year hiatus in the lopsided federalism of devolution. Anyone from the post-devolution generation was fed on the idea that this reborn little country was a progressive beacon that would throw off the shackles of British conservatism and bring about radical social transformation. That was twenty-five years ago; and now the promises of the new political class seem as shallow as the water pooling in the concrete underpasses.

'We're not a leader in the built environment space. We're not reaching the possible', Scott says with a passion that is rare in the bureaucratically sterilised world of city planning. The reality, he emphasises, is that significantly more energy-efficient and sustainable buildings than Glasgow is used to have been very possible for several decades now. We'd first come across each other during the UN climate summit, when there was a clamour to put young Scottish voices front and centre. The problem was that what those voices were asking for jarred with the convenient story of a country at the apex of climate innovation.

Glasgow has just built a new cycle connector down a major street and the council has issued press releases celebrating its own leadership, being careful to make sure the story is visible in what remains of the city's newspapers. Meanwhile the pavements are sinking and the public transport system creaks under the weight of decades of ambivalence. Some cycle lanes and an expensive monthly ticket you can use on any of the privatised buses is the best the council can come up with.

'We wouldn't be pedestrianising streets and paving them; we'd be making green corridors for people to move through, and opening up spaces for people to grow food and socialise', Scott says when I ask him what Glasgow would look like if climate change were being taken seriously. He points to examples from around the world where exactly what we are told is not possible in Glasgow has been done.

The motorway outside takes up about four square kilometres of the city and is falling apart as the 1960s concrete degrades, creating a huge bill for the taxpayer. A campaign has started to turn it into a linear park, alongside a more realistic aim to cap it with a deck to form new public squares. As climate change sets in over the next decade, the pressure on urban infrastructure will grow and grow. Roads are hugely expensive to maintain, and they induce demand that just puts more pressure on city budgets. Walking, on the other hand, is free and the weight of a human foot has around a quarter of the pressure per square inch of a car. Understanding the challenge of climate forces us to look again at the flows of everyday life, people and nature intermingling with weather, energy and history.

Glasgow is a city where angels watch over the streets from Gothic church towers and the carved gutters of sandstone office buildings. Bertrand Tavernier opens *Death Watch* with shots of the Necropolis, the giant Victorian graveyard on a hill accessed across a stone bridge from Glasgow Cathedral, where stone figures look out at the decimation below. It makes Glasgow look like the victim of divine vengeance.

There is a line in the Book of Isaiah that has become a favourite of apocalyptic environmentalists: 'Her towers will be overgrown with thorns, her fortresses with thistles and briers.' It is a threat from God, one that has been paraphrased and mistranslated as the less cumbersome 'Over your cities grass will grow.'

The return of nature has always been associated with the destruction of the city, with the retreat of human life and the fall of civilisation. Yet climate change asks us to embrace the city of thorns. Green avenues, wild neighbourhoods and maintenance and coexistence rather than constant expansion are the future if we are to avoid the ruins entirely. It isn't just about imagining a city without the motorway, but a city without the tarmac sea that chokes the ground and cuts people off from one another.

'We're gonna have to do more together, we're not gonna have endless resources for new buildings', Scott says, pointing to Glasgow's crumbling centre, where the rain falls on silent streets outside office hours, dampening the face of buildings that would be prized as masterpieces of *fin-de-siècle* design by a city with more confidence. 'Once you give people a glimpse of what is possible then people demand it', he says.

Doing nothing is not an option. the average Glaswegian has little idea just how vulnerable the city is to extreme weather. It comes in dribs and drabs and small inconveniences. Leaking roofs, cancelled trains and increased insurance premiums, but the city is still waiting for a major event. That may come sooner rather than later. In Scotland climate change acts as a multiplier for the already stormy weather, and Glasgow is exposed to ocean warming that could lead to flash storms similar to the one that destroyed the suburbs of Valencia, what meteorologists call an atmospheric river, where moisture flows through the air and leads to biblical amounts of rain in an already wet watershed. Where the suburbs of Strathclyde fade into the hills and forests of rural Argyll, the main road over the high passes to the Atlantic coast is regularly washed away by rock and mudslides. The government has spent millions drilling cages and concrete barriers into the rock already, and the bill keeps growing.

Glasgow is built across a series of small rivers flowing towards the Clyde from the north and south. All water eventually falls towards the river before being pushed out to the Irish Sea and the Atlantic. After particularly heavy rains it isn't unusual to see chemical foam floating down on the high water. One of its feeder streams, the Polmadie Burn, is contaminated with chromium leaking from old industrial workings and has turned fluorescent yellow, while the city itself has multiple sites where the groundwater is saturated with industrial pollutants.

After the industry vanished the river was treated as a problem, something that was in the way and needed to be dealt with. The solution was to fill the banks with new roads and shopping centres and to block off public access. The roads served commuter estates filled with homes built by opportunistic developers with bucolic names. Today the Glasgow suburbs are full of cheap brick housing developments with names like Weaver's Brae, Sequoia Meadows and Cornhill Village. Three-, four- and five-bedroom homes for you and your family thrown up by one of the private house-building empires that filled the void created by the public housing crisis and the decimation of the city.

When my parents moved to Glasgow as newlyweds in the early 1980s for Dad's job at the railway shops, they ended up, like so many others, in a brand new suburban house in a small town out of the city. My mum tells a story of stepping off the train for the first time at a station in the bowels of the motorway underpasses the same year that Tavernier's dystopic vision of a city undone was released. She arrived to find rats running down the platform after trains and people sleeping rough in the underpasses as litter blew through the tunnels. City blocks were still being demolished wholesale and Glasgow felt like a country post-invasion, being parcelled up by the victorious powers and the pieces nobody wanted levelled.

Where the River Kelvin falls the last few metres to meet the saltwater of the tidal Clyde is Thornwood, a district of red working-class sandstone tenements that used to run straight into the shipyards at the limit of deep-water navigation. The houses now terminate abruptly at an expressway built to service the 1960s cross-river tunnel, robbed of access to the water.

The approach roads to the tunnel loop up over themselves to direct traffic towards the city centre and its waiting car parks, a Möbius strip that has stolen a corner of the local park. In the 1880s excavations for a new promenade through the park uncovered the fossilised remains of lycopods, huge tree-like mosses that grew as part of coal forests 300 million years ago. The forests in what became Scotland decayed into the Clyde-valley coal seams that were first tapped in Lanarkshire and powered the Industrial Revolution, setting off the chain of events that would culminate in the excavators gouging out four lanes of tarmac through the river bed.

When the lycopods were alive the earth was in the Carboniferous period, the dense forests of ancient life drawing carbon from the atmosphere and storing it, before being crushed under the weight of glaciers they had helped to create by plunging the earth into an ice age. As lycopods and other early forms of flora sucked carbon from the atmosphere they brought about a natural cooling that laid the basis for the emergence of later stages of plant and animal evolution, including humanity. Now the carbon they stored has been released we are heading back towards conditions not seen for millions of years.

Where early amphibians swam in the swamps among lycopod roots, people now sit silently in their cars in the tailbacks that regularly build up around the tunnel. Walking through the park in the shadow of the motorway past the small hut housing the fossil bed, I imagine the steaming mass of roots and swamp that was once there, like Thomas Mann's primal forest in the Munich park.

There are no steaming lycopods here any more and the trees that gave Thornwood its name are gone too, but there is a forest of sorts. Deindustrialisation has strange effects on the natural world and the Clyde Valley is still littered with blocked railway tunnels and half-standing red-brick warehouses that invite life into their damp contours. As Glasgow crumbled throughout the 1970s and 1980s its ex-industrial land began to take on new life devoid of people. Brambles and trees took root in empty city blocks and in the clefts of rusting railway tracks, anchoring themselves in disintegrating buildings and on untended verges. 'Let Glasgow Flourish' is the city's official motto, and flourish it did. It was unintentional, but deindustrialisation began a process of indiscriminate and widespread rewilding as the empty scraps of ground and islands of untended grass grew and merged. In a city robbed of its economy and people, something had to step in.

If you do nothing to abandoned land it goes through stages of natural regeneration. First, weeds break apart tarmac and concrete and widen the cracks of faded brickwork, all part of the semiotic of urban decay. If you wait long enough though, other things begin to happen, a recovery that does not correspond to the impatience of human lifetimes. The unsightly scrub provides cover for trees to grow, and the leaves from the trees enrich the soil. Tree roots break up tarmac and concrete even more, each winter freeze bringing new rounds of reclamation as water freezes and expands, providing ever more space for roots each spring.

Scrubland attracts birds, as well as foxes and urban deer. During the COVID-19 lockdowns, central Glasgow became a ghost town and red deer were spotted wandering up its main shopping street in the middle of the day, what researchers have begun to call the 'anthropause'. As you stand in Thornwood or anywhere else across Glasgow, the city of thorns is only a few months of desertion away.

'The council should be ashamed of themselves', says Bobby, as he adjusts his shirt buttons for me to take his photo on the roundabout with the roar of traffic above us. It's dangerous; the cars file off the expressway and join the merry-go-round before peeling off again to new destinations without paying attention to the two people stepping out from the kerb. The concrete circle is not meant for us, but Bobby has clambered onto it to make a point – the verge in the middle is one of the few patches of green on the street, and he's determined to claim it for locals.

Bobby is the kind of organic intellectual you stumble across fairly regularly in Glasgow, kings of their own small corners of the city raised on the idea that culture is an autonomous right and not something to be given by the better-off. What is perhaps the seminal Glasgow novel – Alasdair Gray's *Lanark* – is a triumph of dystopian fantasy in which Glasgow is transformed into an alternative nightmare city called Unthank. Unthank is a place that owes much to the dark hellscapes of German expressionist cinema, formed from Gray's experience of the black and lightless city in the 1950s and 1960s he witnessed as a young artist struggling for money and desperate to escape.

Gray is known around the world for *Lanark*, but in Glasgow his biggest legacy is his paintings, murals in churches and on buildings, including at the Subway station by the university which shows the Sociology building towering over the neighbourhood. I'm always tempted to add myself in, waving merrily from behind my desk just as Gray did in his own frontispieces for *Lanark*.

Bobby's paintings adorn the local cafés in Thornwood, one of his latest creations a reworking of a Caravaggio featuring himself and other notable Thornwood locals meeting in a coffee shop down the road. Among them is Willy, a Glasgow

University literature professor whom I've often shared a table with in a West End pub, and Stuart, an anarchist arrested on his way to assassinate General Franco in Madrid as part of an ill-conceived autonomous attempt to bring down European fascism. Franco survived for a few decades more, but so, somehow, did Stuart.

Anti-capitalist resistance is not what it once was in Glasgow, as serious-minded reading groups and organised socialism turned to socialising and the simple pleasures of the capitalist leisure economy. Bobby and the other members of the community council are engaged in a more modest war over the location of a new drive-through restaurant by the roundabout. An American burger franchise wants to cut down trees that have sprung up on a small patch of wasteland next to the expressway to build the feeder lane for its new retail site. It doesn't do much to dispel the idea that Scotland's hyped green transformation is less transformative than politicians claim.

'The traffic is so dense – it's the main thoroughfare and the big tenements here create a canyon effect', says Bobby, with a wave of his arms, to accentuate the idea of wind blowing down the street. Suspecting perhaps that I have not fully understood, he imitates the cars on the flyovers rattling the backs of the blocks of flats. 'All the pollutants remain in place, and that isn't going to get any better with this drive-through', he mutters.

The week after I interview Bobby on the roundabout, a motorcade speeds from the airport through Thornwood, carrying Barack Obama, now an ex-president rather than an aspiring one. Since I saw him make his pitch for the future in Berlin the world has added billions of tonnes of new carbon emissions – around 530 billion, to put a figure

on it. The numbers are so large as to be almost meaning-
less. It took until the mid-1970s to create the same level of
emissions from the pre-industrial baseline, and they keep
climbing.

The future of the Thornwood waterfront may well be
academic anyway. Within eighty years, Scotland is anticipated
to experience around half a metre of sea-level rise, according
to the Intergovernmental Panel on Climate Change. The
general rise in sea level, combined with increased rainfall,
will have a catastrophic effect on low-lying cities like
Glasgow. There is talk of new storm drains and setting up
wetland barriers, and even of lifting the entire airport apron
by a few metres, but these are all nothing but scratches on
the skin of the climate monster.

In the middle of the pandemic I was trapped in a small
two-bedroom flat, living alone and teaching students whose
faces I never saw by video call, watching social media flood
with images of the anthropause: crystal-clear canals in Venice,
sheep wandering down from the Welsh hills, smogless skies
over Los Angeles and Beijing, and the deer roaming the
Glasgow streets. Global emissions even temporarily dropped,
and for a brief moment we were given a vision – however
unreal – of a world in which humanity was a fellow traveller
rather than the dominant force on the planet. I was still
regularly getting the miniature seizures that immobilised
the right side of my body, falling into a chemical sleep each
night and unsure whether the series of events that had
unfolded were not just the damaged synaptic flashes of a
comatose brain in a German hospital bed.

I had written something journalistic for the first time in
two and a half years, a short piece for a London magazine

about post-concussive disorders and how poorly understood the brain was. I used to be able to knock eight hundred fairly decent words out in a few hours, but it took me a month, and the words laboured into being where they used to come naturally. I struggled to get a handle on rhythm or diction, going over and over it until I was sure that what was on the page could pass for journalism with a sympathetic editor. Even now, on the days when my brain refuses to play along, I am reminded of the Brazilian novelist Clarice Lispector's lament that reading back her own drafts was like being forced to consume your own vomit. I even have the nausea.

One day I was offered a way out. A house on the west coast that had been sold but needed to be looked after until the money landed in the agent's account. I was made a temporary contractor and given proof of employment so I could travel legally, leaving town almost overnight. I had my pick of hundreds of rental cars sitting in quiet rows at the airport, waiting for mass tourism to return, driving west through the February snows to four thousand acres of land and a house on the shores of an Argyll sea loch where it emptied into the Atlantic. A faded mansion with its own walled garden and grand driveway, the old manse needed its fires lit and the perimeter fence walking to keep out the exploding population of Japanese deer and to stop the roof degrading any further.

I knew very little about the place when I took the gig, stopping only to check that I could get a phone signal to upload online lectures and check emails and to get a double prescription of nerve suppressants from the pharmacist. The house was down a gravel track off a minor road that splits from the main highway down the Mull of Kintyre. There were a few cottages on the estate but nobody had lived in the main house for years, and the water supply was unusable, contaminated by the acidic peat. I'd been warned it would be safer to wash and shower either in the loch or using boiled water collected in a cistern. When I pulled the car up and saw it for the first time in the fading light it seemed intensely familiar, and sure enough, the taps in the kitchen ran rust-brown as promised. The deer grazed on the far reaches of the lawn, together with a few sheep who had migrated along the shoreline at low tide.

The house was under offer from one of the heirs to an Anglo-Irish drinks dynasty, with the time and money to turn it back into an aristocratic home. I lit the fire in the study and drawing room, and stepped outside to get my bearings in the gloam as the snow began to fall on the high ground of Kintyre across the loch. From the end of the headland by the house you can look out to the farm on Jura where George Orwell wrote *Nineteen Eighty-Four*, coping with the disease that would soon kill him and desperate to escape and work divorced from the world. Orwell had no hire cars or 4G internet and no Zoom calls, but he lived in a world where tuberculosis was as deadly as COVID-19 and London and Glasgow alike were thick with coal dust and carbon monoxide.

As I settled in I began to walk around the headland every day and back along the north shore, where the seals play, watching the empty boats headed for Islay and Jura with no passengers on deck skirt the sandbars in the loch. One day as I walked up from watching seabirds off the old pier in the late afternoon, I caught the manse at a certain angle and realised why I already knew it. It was the house from *Death Watch*.

As the film builds to a crescendo, Harvey Keitel and Romy Schneider head to the sea in search of Schneider's ex-husband, portrayed by the Swedish actor Max von Sydow, most famous for facing down death over a game of chess on the beach in Ingmar Bergman's *Seventh Seal*, or as the villain in the camp adaptation of *Flash Gordon* from the early 1980s or in David Lynch's cult adaptation of *Dune*. In *Death Watch* von Sydow is a hermit, alone in the half-abandoned mansion with a gramophone, surrounded by books and divorced from the horror of the world at large as well as his ex-wife.

I downloaded the film on the shaky mobile internet connection and watched it through in short bursts, stopping to check each scene. Every space was identical, down to the titles on the shelves and the faded yellow wallpaper in the hallway. Sticking my head into the abandoned dining room, the furniture the actors had sat on was stacked under dust sheets, the curtains folded in piles on top. It was a flash of a time when the house was maintained and full of life, before the slates had slipped in the winter storms and the damp had set in to the wallpaper in the drawing room. Each day I unwittingly re-created the drama as a form of ritual, knowing in which chairs the actors had sat and the angles of light as it came into the study, where Tavernier would have waited all day to get the shot he needed. The city was far away and there I was, acting out the final scenes of Glasgow's apocalyptic fantasy.

The temptation to run away never leaves you, especially when you're ill, as if you can step outside disease and become a different person through sheer force of will. Since the Industrial Revolution environmentalists have sought out wilderness and the old ways to combat the attrition of everyday life, the richer ones turning Britain's countryside into little Ruritanian idylls that exist only when the owners are present. Whoever has bought the house will be doing the same, leaving their office or London flat for the evening flight to Glasgow and the drive out west. After the pandemic the price of property in rural Scotland skyrocketed as people realised they could trade in unglamorous London addresses for entire farms. A friend's brother, aged 32, retired to the Central Highlands after making enough money in tech and the London housing market to fund him for the rest of his existence.

Eventually I have to abandon my one-man drama and head back east to pick up books and more brain medication from the chemist. Waiting on the mat is six weeks of unopened mail and the appointment letter for another trip for an MRI scan, so I clamber in the car and head out into the weather front that has blown in over the Hebrides.

The rain closes the pass between Argyll and the Lowlands again. Mudslides have swamped the tarmac and trucks sit upended in ditches after being tipped over by the wind. Driving back towards Glasgow, the roads get bigger and the air thicker with noise until I am filing dutifully past super-markets and retail parks that seem out of time. They are condemned to become relics, like the factories and railway marshalling yards they replaced.

If you read on from the bible passage that promises a city of thorns, the divine vengeance is followed by the spectre of birds of prey making their nests in the ruins in the post-human landscape. I think of the falcons in the university bell tower, who see different maps, of a city outside human time where the contours of the rivers and hills become the primary reference points and the changes in the wind direction dictate life. I think of my mum, four decades ago, stepping across newspapers blowing in the backdraft from the railway tunnels into a city on its knees, of Tavernier's empty streets and drifting refugees, and the steaming lycopod forest that became the foundation of the city of furnaces burning on the dark plain. It crumbles in the afterglow with the thorns bursting from the cracks.

5

The atomic coast

The sun is not yet up and the only light, an artificial glow from the line of street lamps stretching from the main road to the shoreline, lacks warmth. The December wind blows off the sea and into the line of people in identical high-vis safety jackets filing towards the heavily guarded main gate. A few stray snowflakes escaped from their clouds dance briefly under the LED bulbs. It is undeniably midwinter.

Ahead of me razor wire and armed police wait, and behind them the silhouette of Dounreay's reactors in the fading starlight of an Atlantic dawn. This is an almost mythical place, a mausoleum for the dreams of technological optimism and a cautionary tale about the long tail of quickly made decisions. An experimental nuclear power station bolted to the rock of the north coast, Dounreay is a place I thought I would never see for myself.

'I don't think you realise how lucky you are to be standing here', says Linda, walking by my side into the security hut. The nuclear police pop their heads in and chat to the receptionist, turning to note our presence on the benches. Spending the small days before Christmas in a high-security nuclear site in the north of Scotland is not an experience many people would jump at.

I first met Linda in a crowded bar in Glasgow before the pandemic. She is an historian of rural modernism and energy, and an expert on Dounreay. She has a love of the concrete buildings, bridges, dams and water towers strung out across the Highlands. Where we see picturesque wilderness, she sees a technological landscape full of social change. It was by chance that we both found ourselves up in Caithness at the same time, doing fieldwork from budget hotel rooms and the backs of cars that should have been scrapped long ago.

Waiting at the checkpoint is Magnus, a go-to point man in the far north of Scotland who has been on national and international news as an unofficial ambassador for Caithness and its potential. He's a talented researcher who was sensible enough to leave the hustle of academia and move to work at Dounreay, where the workday ends at five and the lifestyle is more sustainable. He knows everyone and everything in town.

Until the Second World War Dounreay was coastal farmland around a small village of the same name, part of the small pocket of good pasture in Caithness that marks the little triangular province out from the high hills of the Scottish Highlands. It would have stayed that way, but in 1945 the British government found itself unexpectedly locked out of the American nuclear programme it had helped to create, and so began Dounreay's unlikely place in world history.

The world's first functioning nuclear reactor had been built by the Italian physicist Enrico Fermi under a sports stadium at the University of Chicago. There was an assumption in London that after the war ended Britain and the US would pool their resources in harnessing the power of atomic energy. In reality, the US had other ideas, and Britain suddenly had to develop both an independent nuclear deterrent and its own energy programme at short notice, pulling together domestic engineers and nuclear physicists to make it happen. An inventory of state assets showed that Dounreay, with a railhead and a port nearby, was the place to do it.

Getting past the Dounreay gate means agreeing to take no photos and make no notes or recordings. I've been through security clearance and a background check, and told them my history of radiation exposure. It's three decades since any energy has been generated at Dounreay, but shortly after our visit it's announced that the site will carry on operating until 2070. Nuclear clean-up is difficult enough at the best of times, but Dounreay was an experimental facility and things were done quickly in the name of scientific progress. Nothing was standardised, and nobody had thought about what would happen when the time came to switch off the reactors. Picking apart the nuclear legacy is like dismantling a haystack straw by straw.

When Dounreay's first test reactor came online in 1956 it was heralded as a breakthrough in nuclear technology and a triumph of British engineering. Britain flirted with the idea of a nuclear-powered future using domestic technology pioneered on the north coast of Scotland, not just nuclear power stations but ships and even space rockets running on the effectively limitless energy it promised. In the 1950s nuclear technology was pitched as part of a bright future free from rumbling coal trains and dirty furnaces, full of easy leisure and clean air.

Radioactive elements have unstable nuclei; when bombarded with neutrons they come apart more willingly than the rest of the periodic table. Long before Enrico Fermi built his functioning reactor there is evidence that the process had already happened in waterlogged uranium deposits in

West Africa, where natural springs had acted as a moderator in nuclear chain reactions. The challenge with the early experiments in nuclear energy was not to start a reaction, but to keep it going, and to then turn the released energy into electricity.

In the 1950s geologists were still unsure how much uranium would be easily obtained from the earth's crust. Like the anxieties about exhausting global oil and coal supplies, the pioneers of nuclear energy had not factored in that our ability to locate and mine the element would grow exponentially. Dounreay was designed to produce more than it consumed by creating plutonium that could replace uranium as the primary fuel for the nuclear programme, giving Britain energy independence and freedom from volatile overseas energy sources.

Today Dounreay wears its history lightly, feeling more like an industrial estate than one of the most advanced nuclear facilities in the world. We move through a tarmac-scape of warehouses and car parks, passing office blocks and canteens. Over the fence is a Royal Navy site for testing nuclear-submarine reactors. The police are conducting security drills all around us, with coloured tape attached to the end of their machine guns to show they are firing blanks. We pass through their simulated terror attack like ghosts.

We strip to our underwear and put on overalls with radiation monitors clipped to the breast pocket. Then the screening staff usher us on through an airlock and into a cavernous hall, now largely empty, containing the remains of Dounreay's prototype fast reactor. Scaffolding and steel gangways criss-cross the floor, and from the edge of the platform we peer down into the remains of the reactor itself.

The sarcophagus is sealed, opened only when extraction is taking place using robots and remote drills. When the

Dounreay site was taken offline the sodium in the fast reactor turned from liquid to solid, forming a hard irradiated crust that needs to be chipped away. It is one of the reasons the plant is still teeming with people, hundreds of technicians and nuclear scientists trying to solve problems inadvertently created in the rush for clean energy.

Nuclear reactions produce a series of new isotopes which remain highly radioactive long after the reactor is taken offline, and anything that gets irradiated along the way also needs to be dealt with. Everything that has been used in the reactor or that has been exposed to it becomes functionally useless, right down to everyday items like ballpoint pens and watches, rivets, spanners and overalls. Once exposed to radiation, objects are subject to a kind of metaphysical transfiguration – their very essence changes. Banal everyday items suddenly become dangerous artefacts of the nuclear age. Atomic clean-up means thinking about legacies lasting far longer than any human lifespan.

Up a metal stairwell our guide – a man who has served his whole career at Dounreay – introduces us to the handlers, the men and women whose job it is to work with the most dangerous relics of Dounreay's early days. I can't name any of the people we meet but you could bump into them in a pub in town or the supermarket. These are highly skilled manual jobs that pay well. Getting a job at the plant is seen as a good prospect for people in Caithness and Sutherland. The handlers walk up and down a gallery known colloqui- ally as the Cave, stopping to operate huge mechanical arms that perfectly mimic the movement of human hands behind radiation-shielded glass. They move not just the spent nuclear fuel but the mundane irradiated objects too. In one of the chambers I see a series of bolts that are being separated one by one from their casings and placed in secure drums.

Nothing is allowed to get away. Nobody in the room will live to see the time when the containerised waste is no longer a danger.

Trains of nuclear material leave Caithness for England carrying relics of the white heat of technology. The wagons that carry the lead-lined nuclear flasks are specially built, always pulled by two locomotives with armed nuclear police riding in the rear cabs. Unlisted on public timetables, taking the waste by rail is far safer than flying it or taking it by road. The government tried to allay public concern about accidents in the 1980s by running an empty express train into the flask wagons at top speed and filming it. The front of the diesel locomotive simply disintegrates but once the dust has settled, the nuclear container emerges from the wreckage intact.

'Just be careful, it's a bit cold inside because of the vacuum', says the supervisor taking us through the airlock into Dounreay's second reactor.

We're entering the Sphere, the huge dome visible from miles around that was built to house Dounreay's other energy-producing experimental reactor. The Sphere is so iconic it's used as the logo for the site itself – no name is needed on the branded notepaper and pens we are given. Whichever angle you come from the dome is there, lit up in the dusk by the setting sun and the orange glow of the plant itself.

The unique shape was used to avoid having any weak points – the similarity to the spaceships of post-war science fiction is not just coincidental. When Stanley Kubrick wanted to make 2001: A Space Odyssey he asked NASA engineers to design realistic large spacecraft that would be able to resist the interior pressure in a vacuum, and their solution was spheres that look remarkably like the Dounreay reactor hall.

If something were to go wrong the Sphere was intended to contain it. Around the perimeter there are escape chutes leading to one-way airlocks, but instead of falling into a waiting escape pod to be jettisoned into space, anyone fleeing will find themselves in the drifting rain of the Caithness winter. The Sphere is an anachronistic mixture of contemporary and 1950s tech, computer screens and modern control equipment jacked into the original consoles. The floor is stacked high with temporary rigs and scaffolding to dismantle the reactor. The latest issue the clean-up team have come across is fuel rods jammed in their casings, and the engineers are busy designing tools that can get them out.

Nobody working at the site now was there in the early days when many of the biggest errors were made, but Dounreay has fought a constant battle with public opinion, and anti-nuclear campaigners regularly protest against shipments to the south of the UK or by air to the US from the local airport. The UK's stockpile of nuclear warheads is kept in a bunker drilled into the hillside on Loch Long just outside Glasgow and is completely separate from the decommissioning work, but opposition to nuclear weapons has often also meant opposition to nuclear energy on Scottish soil. Ask anyone local, however, and they will almost without exception speak positively about Dounreay and its legacy.

The answers here are not simple. Nuclear power is dangerous, but coal and oil are deadly in more subtle ways. I remember sitting on the Shinkansen bullet train back to Tokyo in Japan after a visit to Fukushima Daichi – the scene of one of the world's worst nuclear disasters, where the region still bears the scars of the nuclear contamination. Fukushima's cleanup is still ongoing, but it was an incoming tsunami from the Pacific that destroyed whole towns. The meltdown came after. The cyclones and typhoons of climate change make the risks of nuclear energy look manageable as a bridge to full decarbonisation, even if the truth is complex. Karin, the guide and translator who had shown me round Fukushima, had told me how Japanese summers were beginning to become unbearably hot the further south you travelled through Honshu. In Fukushima, people were wary about being labelled as the Japanese Chernobyl, struggling too with heat-impacted rice harvests and a lack of rain. The people working around Fukushima were forthright about their frustration at how the place had become a media trope and a political football.

Scotland has so much green energy that nuclear stations could never compete, but that is not true everywhere. Climate change forces us into uncomfortable trade-offs and negotiations with our own future. Japan is not Scotland, and Dounreay has a different lesson in a country trying to wean itself off fossil fuels. When the reactors were taken offline in the early 1990s, the outlook was bleak and Caithness braced for a shrinking population and an exodus of professional jobs, just as the North Sea oil towns are doing now. What had not been factored in was the long cost of decommissioning. Each year the government in London pumps millions into the local area in direct and indirect subsidies. Just two years of Dounreay's annual budget is bigger than the entire Shetland oil fund. It is exactly what the rest of the country needs.

* * *

If you drive out of Dounreay and inland you quickly come to open ground devoid of farms, houses and people. This is the Flow Country, the name for the high moors of bog and heather that start just behind the coast and run up into the mountains of Sutherland. This is – according to environmental campaigners and nature writers at least – Britain's last wilderness, muted browns and pastel greens stretching for miles across a treeless landscape where the open ground provides little protection from the sheets of rain drifting in from the coast. There are few roads up here and often not a building to be seen, but this is an empty place by design.

One of the first times I met Magnus it was summer and he had agreed to be interviewed about renewable energy and peat restoration in the flows. He pulled up in a jeep three times the size of my little Japanese car and we left Thurso to drive up gravel tracks to one of the small lochs where the River Thurso begins, from where we set off on foot. Magnus wanted to show me the scars of Caithness's past, the ruins that sit deep in the cultural memory of what happens when a community is laid waste. We hiked up over the high ground of the east with the North Sea on one side and the Sutherland hills on the other, drowning in midges in the late afternoon. You could feel the moisture rising from the bog, wet above and wet below.

When the world shut down during the coronavirus pandemic Magnus set out to visit and map all the lost communities of the Flow Country on foot, scattered crofting townships dotting the landscape that were inhabited as late as the 1950s. Before diesel and petrol cars transformed the interior of Sutherland, people would walk, sometimes twenty miles at a time, from township to township or down the strath to the towns. The Flow Country has just been made a World Heritage Site in recognition of its complex system of blanket peat bogs; as far as the UN are concerned this is one of the world's biggest carbon banks, part of a global accounting system alongside the Amazon and the Florida Everglades that is trying to maintain and expand the best natural methods of greenhouse gas removal.

Magnus pointed to a ruin on the hillside. 'That was a school ... and over there you can see the remains of a township.' I asked him why the school was so isolated. 'It's halfway between the townships', he said. The Flows were a functioning linear community for hundreds of years. Up on the Flows it is easy to spot eagles soaring on the thermals, and flying over in a small plane you can make out the ruined foundations of buildings hidden in grass and heather, and trace the old tracks that linked them.

The restoration of the peatlands is sponsored by the government and several large conservation charities, and on the map Caithness and Sutherland are a promised land for metropolitan conservationists who desperately want a British Alaska. Magnus does not agree. The obsession with rewilding the Far North (even the 'Far' is disliked by a lot of Caithness people, the product of a map seen from the bottom of Britain) is a failure to imagine landscapes where nature, people and high technology coexist.

'There's no reason why these places shouldn't be repopulated', Magnus told me that day on the hill. 'We can build modern energy-efficient homes, we can power them with renewable energy, and we have jobs for them to go to.'

He doesn't mince his words about what the North needs and what it can do. It's easy to see why he's popular in the county.

In the centre of Thurso are the public offices of Nuclear Restoration Services (NRS), the public agency that now runs Dounreay. Across the street is an exhibition in the town museum where rainy-day visitors lift Perspex fuel rods from a plywood reactor using the same metal arms as in the Cave, but without the risk of a slow death.

A cruise ship carrying German tourists has just arrived in the harbour and apprentices from Dounreay with the familiar Sphere on their backs hand out information packs about Thurso. The Germans wander the streets looking for knitwear and Celtic jewellery, suspiciously eyeing the local cakes in the bakery windows and walking out of a café that only serves filter coffee as they hunt for macchiatos. The NRS has provided money towards upgrading the port and local infrastructure with a new pier and loading ramps to help fishermen and the renewables industry, but the cruise ships benefit too. They used to just sail straight past on their way to more famous places. Under the government cutbacks of the last fifteen years the NRS has been a lifeline for Thurso.

I'm back in town, at Magnus's suggestion, to meet Dorothy, a crofter from one of the crofting communities that sit on the north coast. The Mhoine peninsula is an hour's drive west past the nuclear plant and into the higher ground of Sutherland, where it cuts down to meet the Atlantic. Dorothy is identifiably a local – Caithness and Sutherland have a distinctive accent that has begun to fade as outlying villages suffer from depopulation and people drop their dialect.

Carry on past the Mhoine towards Cape Wrath at the far north-western tip of the island of Great Britain and elaborate eco-homes built by incomers sit alongside abandoned croft houses and luxury tourist accommodation for £150 a night. Locals struggle to afford housing, and there are a dwindling number of children here. Dorothy is a retired schoolteacher. When she locked up her classroom for the last time there were just fourteen on the roll.

Melness is the township on the eastern side of the Mhoine where it touches the Kyle of Tongue, a huge sea inlet with a natural dune system and tidal flats that pushes inland until it meets bare rock at the base of the hills. In midwinter the sun goes down in the south behind the craggy twin peaks of Ben Loyal, one of the two northernmost mountains in Scotland, looking out over the Atlantic from 2,500 feet. The views from the top are spectacular, to Orkney, over to the Outer Hebrides, and beyond that towards Iceland and Greenland.

Melness is not like the other communities strung out along the north coast. Balanced on the low cliffs above golden beaches, it is owned by the crofters whose houses run along the shore, giving them a modicum of control that others in the Highlands do not enjoy. The estate used to be a private holding like any other, with a laird and tenants who paid an annual rent. By a stroke of luck the community was gifted the land by a benevolent owner with no interest in running a human zoo, just as the Scottish land-reform movement was taking hold in the 1990s. The banner on the crofters' website reads 'A place bereft of people is a soulless place.' On the home page is a picture of Dorothy sitting on the beach by her home, staring out at the sea.

'Because we don't have a landlord, we can make that decision', says Dorothy. I think of Mick behind the desk in the mining club in Coalburn, with his spreadsheets and maps, trying to claw back favours and windfalls from energy giants to help the shrinking village around him.

'Melness is building twelve houses just now, but that will be for local people', Dorothy says proudly. It's an unambiguous slight at the tourist traps further up the coast where the road is thick with luxury jeeps in high summer but empty of traffic the rest of the time. I'm almost driven off the road west later that day by a luxury camper on raised suspension coming around the corner. The north coast is heavily marketed as a must-see that competes with wilderness holidays in Iceland and Costa Rica for space on the advertising hoardings of the London Underground. None of the advertisements mention the people in the wilderness. My microphone runs out of battery without warning and I pull out my phone so she can continue.

Most of the Mhoine is low-grade grazing land, heather and bog rising up from the back of the croft houses that the average passer-by would see as barren and desolate. Used for letting sheep and cattle roam, it's well suited to its other use, as Scotland's first spaceport.

The phrase conjures images of spaceplanes ready on the runway and passengers preparing for a trip into orbit, of Kubrick's spherical lander touching down on the moon. The truth is more prosaic. With support from the NRS and in partnership with a commercial space company based outside Inverness, the crofters are building a site for small-scale commercial launches over the open sea to the north.

I mention the word rewilding to Dorothy, and how the push to bring back 'nature' sits alongside the crofters' ambitions to blast rockets into orbit. There' considerable opposition to the idea of a space-launch site and the spectre of rockets in the skies over the wilderness that many want the North to be. People who've never been to Sutherland and who perhaps never will sign petitions, thinking they're protecting a pristine habitat. The adjoining land is owned by a Danish fast-fashion magnate who has bankrolled much of the activism. He's opposed the spaceport on the grounds that it does not fit with his vision of Sutherland and the open Atlantic fringe.

'I don't want to hear the word rewilding', reacts Dorothy, 'Our land has been managed by crofters for generations. Even with the spaceport project we're doing peat restoration. It's been described as pristine. To have somebody come in and say we're going to rewild it is very patronising.'

When tourists come to the north coast looking for space, this is perhaps not what they mean, but Melness is the centre of a nascent space industry that builds on the seventy years of high technology on the North Coast that began with the nuclear plant. The area around Dounreay has more highly skilled jobs than anywhere else in the North of Scotland. The spaceport will bring some of those skills west into Sutherland, but it's also a statement of intent about a sustainable future in which the north coast is not just a rich city person's annual playground.

Caithness is a place some never even stop, or if they do it's because they can't go any further. Reaching the top of Scotland is anticlimactic for those who imagine they are going to the ends of the earth, only to find supermarkets, big farms and people busy living everyday life. Travel bloggers post videos about visiting the most northerly point in Britain and the wild majesty of the Flows. They move on to Orkney without any mention of Thurso, but the real mark of the place is in the bars in town and down at the harbour, the Indian restaurants on a Friday night and the high-street tea shops, of people coming off shift at the plant and pouring into warm rooms. Linda and I have chatted long about how we like it here off season, a real place rather than a tourist-fever dream.

We drive out west again, past Dounreay and up through the small winding glen of Strath Halladale, crowned by glacial moraines and flanked by pine plantations. It's a tautology: *strath* and *dale* are the Gaelic and Norse words for the same thing, but the names of the landscape merely show how people are just passing through in the grand scheme of things. The Vikings and the Celts were both passers-by, now visible only in their words and stone ruins.

We get out at Forsinard, high in the flows, where the restoration of the peat is already well advanced. The ponds that dot the site are frozen so solid you could walk on them. On the boardwalk the ice crystals have begun to sprout upwards, unsupported, with no wind or snow to shape them. In the gloam the lights in the signal box at the lonely railway station grow brighter against the washed-out sky and the breeze drops off to silence.

The walk across the bog is slippery, on crunching planks to a little wooden tower that sits alone like a lighthouse among the pools. I always come back here when I can, climbing the tower to sit on the platform at the top and stare out at the rolling peaks across the wet expanse. When you stand here and look out across the landscape you can see thousands of years laid out in front of you, and the thousand years to come, a reminder that the flows of energy and carbon over millennia are bigger than the short chronology in which we live. This is a window into deeper time, the coal and nuclear age alike vanishing against the backdrop of the Sutherland mountains and the stars of the western sky.

Soon the tell-tale flare of rocket engines will sparkle over the Atlantic as the crofters of Melness assemble to watch, in the late light, a flash in the northern chill above the peat flows. Dounreay will sit there in its long retirement, slowly being detoxified and made safe. In a century it will become a quiet museum to the few short decades of technological optimism that made it, and to the society it helped create.

We turn and go back to the car, inching down the icy roads towards the sea as the light fails. In the headlights deer stalk the horizon and the night begins to close around us, falling downwards into the future as the world drifts slowly on.

6

The tidal race

Kirsteen hands me a mug of tea and Callum adjusts himself on the sofa cushions. He's wearing his blue University of Glasgow engineering hoodie, not out of deference to the visitor but because the eastern Highlands are in the grip of a winter freeze. We're in the living room of a Victorian villa in Dingwall, outside Inverness, on the old road north that loops around the heads of the Beauly and Cromarty firths. The clock is not far past three but it is already as good as dark.

I know Kirsteen and Callum because of a death, a mutual friend lost during the pandemic, aged just 36. I never used to understand people who said ageing was a gift, but when you see lives cut off mid-flow you become acutely aware of the ways in which we can be robbed of the future we thought was ours and that there's no logic of justice to it. Here in the freezing late afternoon in the Highlands it feels as if we're giving an extended wake for the departed.

It's strange to sit with people who you know only because of the absence of someone else, but shared memory is also a means of moving on. It helps us structure time, and our meetings with each other work as mileposts as we progress from the past to the future. Our social lives are marked, as

Ted Hughes said, by moments in which we remember others by the degree of feeling they can register, the voltage of life they can carry and tolerate. The tiny explosions of energy in our brain give life feeling.

'Don't be a stranger', Kirsteen had said to me when we parted the first time, so here I am, eyeing the frost on the windows, sitting on the big cushions in the lounge with the two cats and my mug of black tea. She and Callum came to Dingwall to find space for a pandemic baby that grew into a toddler and now a small boy, following the offer of good work in the renewables boom with one of the big international companies. The electric heaters are on, six warm hearts beating in a warm room as the world outside creaks softly under the weight of afternoon frost.

Callum works as a project developer speccing sites for potential new wind farms. The green energy explosion has been felt most keenly in the Eastern Highlands, where the land is more developed and the grid easier to access than further west amongst the real mountains. The family were only too happy to go where the turbines were and where the investors were directing their money. Within a thirty-kilometre radius of the house there are already enough turbines to power a small city, and soon there will be enough to power a large one. On the drive up I've been kept company by the main grid connector running along the trunk road north. The pylons make possible a shift in how energy is produced that most people will never see or think about as they charge their phones on the kitchen sideboard.

The turbines are not uncontroversial – their opponents claim they ruin pristine highland views and kill rare birds, and the more conspiracy-minded share dubious facts about the vibrations and noise disrupting sleep, anecdotal stories of cancer hotspots and waves of chronic fatigue. This stretch of the east coast has a reputation for incomers pitching up only to find an existing community more interested in jobs and keeping their libraries and medical services than the call of the wild. It also has a reliable roster of waifs and cranks – Inverness is one of the centres of a global conspiracy movement. All the way up the A9 from Edinburgh someone has sprayed 'Flat Earth' on the road signs. The flat-earthers had their own shop in the city centre for a while, drawing people in with the promise of truths nobody else was brave enough to tell. It closed quietly a few years ago, but the spray paint still appears in the middle of the night.

This part of the east is dominated by the three huge sea inlets of the North Sea, the Beauly Firth, the Dornoch Firth and Cromarty Firth. They start well inland and run out to the deeper water of the coast, forming a natural barrier that isolates the far north of Scotland from the rest of the country. Go west and you hit the mountains proper, but up the coast clusters of smelters, oil and wind fabrication yards and small factories run in a line up from Inverness to Dornoch. This little strip of coastline is a linear industrial town of over thirty thousand people masquerading as countryside.

There are those who come to escape the future and those who come to build it. Renewables have led to a different kind of incomer to the conservative retirees and spiritualists – younger, university educated and invested in the renewable economy, they are here to build the New Scotland™. When Callum got the chance to move up, Kirsteen went to work for a research company that develops energy-efficient and low-carbon buildings. They are the bit of the national good-news story that holds up to scrutiny.

Wind engineers are not the first to pull power from the glens. After the Second World War the British government undertook a massive expansion of hydroelectric power in Scotland, huge dams under public ownership generating electricity that helped to create jobs for returning servicemen and delivered clean energy to the coasts. The dams and reservoirs are now as much part of the landscape as the hill summits and the forests, huge storage batteries in the shadow of the ridges waiting to be turned on when needed. A generation of men now vanishing were christened the hydro boys, pouring the towering reinforced concrete spillovers and blasting tunnels through the mountainsides with dynamite and handheld pneumatic drills. Some were still in their teens, sharing the back of trucks with men five years their senior who had survived deployment to Europe and the invasion of Germany and Italy, who had killed and seen true horror and wanted nothing more than to come home and live well.

Climate change is a different kind of war; there are no gangs of shirtless men covered in concrete dust and blasting sirens wailing; instead the turbines arrive by sea and then on trucks, supervised by university-trained engineers in hard hats and reflective jackets like Callum. Software maps wind speeds and elevations, working out how air currents circulate around mountain ridges and the potential power outputs based on long-range weather forecasts. Algorithms tell investors how long it will be until a project breaks even and what the likely returns are over its lifetime, averaging energy prices against the wind-flow models and running costs.

'It made sense to be where it was happening', Callum says, from his perch on the edge of the sofa. 'Why sit in a flat in Edinburgh when you can have a house, be close to where you need to be and surrounded by mountains?'

The boy, Seóras, is already in his pyjamas as he mounts the first step of the wooden staircase, too light to make it creak. The darkness is now total. The shortest day is only a week away. He patters onto the landing, bound by the night and the childish time of a world that shrinks in winter and has infinite borders in summer. The cats snuggle further into the carpet, and I step outside onto the gravel of the driveway and into the chill. The car thermometer shows minus seven with ice beginning to glisten in the cavities of the tarmac on the road to the railway station. The windscreen is already white, and I run the engine for a few minutes, sitting in the driver's seat in my thick jacket bought to survive a Scandinavian winter, my breath visible in front of me. In the night, turbines punch the frigid air in three-point rhythm, turning the breeze into heat and light.

I drive on north through the stars, alone on the road with Polaris hanging in the wind above Sutherland and Caithness and the ice crystals fighting a war with the heater around the edge of the windscreen. The wind picks up and I check the service information for the ferry that shuttles back and forth from the tip of mainland Scotland to Orkney. On top of the pocket of cold air another storm is closing in and they have already emailed a warning that the sailings might be cancelled.

Six o'clock feels like midnight as empty roads take me, always longer and further than you think, until the bright car deck of the boat beckons in the port in Thurso and I am waved on. The bow visor folds down behind, sealing us in against the world, and the engines under the car deck grind into life.

By the time I reach Kirkwall, Orkney's capital, the rain circles around the houses and the wind is coming in strong from the east, rocking the orange lifeboat at the quayside. Kirkwall harbour is a mishmash of fishing boats, yachts and the local ferries that connect the town to the remote outer islands. I duck into a bar on the harbour road and the roar is cut off by the draught seal on the door like a speaker that has suddenly lost its input. The bass hum of the air around the building is superseded by glasses and chatter, people swapping lonely living rooms for the sociability of the pub until they're kicked out and told to go home.

I'm waiting for a familiar face, and a few minutes later she comes in. Sarah is a touch older than me but ageless in the way some academics seem to end up as they sidestep conventional lives, a flick of white-blonde hair and the tell-tale glow of an open cold-water swimmer. She's a naturalised Orcadian by way of Glasgow and Missouri who lives some of the year on one of the outlying islands to the south. She travels between the city and the archipelago with a curious dachshund called Lefebvre, named after the French sociologist, who likes to sniff the cardboard boxes and kit bags under my office sofa.

'I'm afraid I can't stay long; they might be closing the barriers', she says as she sits down. Orkney is strung together by a series of coastal barrages down its east side that effectively make the central island – Mainland – a third bigger and put the villages of the south within commuting distance of the capital. Built on the remains of wartime submarine defences, on their inward side they create a huge calm harbour in the protected waters of Scapa Flow. The seaward edges see rollers breaking on the boulders at their base that can easily swamp the road. The water is peppered with the black shadows of rusting hulks just under the surface.

The night looks less and less inviting as the wall clock ticks above the bar and I'm glad that I'm at the hotel five doors down, with its generator, gas boiler, instant hot water and central heating. If the power goes out on the outer isles people still need to turn to camping stoves and hand torches. Energy is precarious, even in the supposed heart of the renewables revolution.

Sarah gives me advice on things to look at while I'm in Orkney. She's an expert on the Orcadian film director Margaret Tait, the first woman in Scotland to ever direct a feature film and a groundbreaking self-described 'film poet', who along with the novelist George Mackay Brown, helped to put Orkney on the cultural map. Tait trained at film school in Rome after abandoning a career as an army doctor and used the islands as the building blocks for her language of experimental cinema, mixing texture, words and landscape on screen. She only ever made one feature film – *Blue Black Permanent* – which became a cult object among film students in the days before art films were freely available on the internet, and a keystone reference for other female directors and landscape poets. Lately her work has been going through a renaissance as a new generation of filmmakers and cinematographers find inspiration in it, oblique references and nods popping up in mainstream releases if you know where to look.

Tait used layered narratives to explore memory, trauma and inheritance. The sea around Orkney becomes an intergenerational band, a constant in a world of change and a font of both death and liberation. Her films are dreams within dreams woven together by colour and sound.

I first came to Orkney tagging along with an American anthropologist, piggybacking on a research trip at his invitation to break the monotony of meals taken alone in unfamiliar cheap hotels and roadside cafés that come with academic fieldwork. That day in baking sun we walked the high road up above Scapa Flow to get an aerial view of the wrecks and the oil terminal on its southern edge. At the time I didn't know that Orkney would keep drawing me back, but the streets of the archipelago's tiny twin cities are known now. I can float through the pubs, the cafés and the hideaways, and run into people I half-know. It's a homely place.

I came to Orkney just after the accident, in the dark months before the pandemic hit. When I could hardly use a computer or drive a car without the taste of metal on my tongue and the right side of my body seizing up, I let the train take me to places I hoped might push me towards recovery, rolling through a cold Highland dusk to the end of the line and waiting for the Orkney boat under the swaying streetlights of the mainland port. In Stromness a local journalist friend drove me around to tend to her horses and walk the beaches, a long way from work and the city, from the MRI scanners and emails from human resources telling me my sick pay had run out. It was the first furthest I'd travelled since coming back from Germany for treatment, still living in a waking dream. I stood on the open sea buffeted by the easterlies, feeling alive with energy in my fingertips even as my brain waded through thick oil.

The beaches of Orkney are a good place to feel small. Personal crisis seems irrelevant in landscapes moulded by older and deeper forces. Tait was captivated by the relationship between landscape and time, not just nature but the slow-moving hyperobjects that shape the world. There is a concept from her film poem *Now* that sits with me, what she calls a unity of time and place with other times and places. It's a pushback against the simplistic chronologies through which we're taught to see our lives, of events happening and moving to their conclusion in neat, quick circles of short human time with clear causes and instant solutions. You don't need to spend long in Orkney to realise that the sea, the wind and the light are in constant interplay, and Tait saw a world

populated and formed by ghosts and relics, all speaking to
one another across hundreds, thousands and millions of years.

Sarah leaves to rescue Lefebvre from the back of the car
and I head to the empty bar in the hotel and sink a whisky
and swallow some pills, attempting to head off what feels
like the beginnings of a migraine. That night I can't sleep
because of the wind; when I close my eyes there are flashes
of colour across my vision that come and go. The shape of
the bedside lamp lingers after it's been turned off, the elec-
tromagnetic spectrum sitting somewhere deep in the inner
landscape of my brain. When I wake up I find a message
from Sarah; she's made it home, one of the last cars through
before the police closed the barriers and the storm set in
fully.

After I asked about renewables contacts beyond the big
operators Sarah had given me the name of a neighbour down
in South Ronaldsay, who in turn gave me the name of a
friend who they thought I should talk to, a woman working
in community renewables back over in Stromness on the
Atlantic side of Orkney. Stromness is a town you can walk
the length of in ten minutes, a single long street of stone
houses facing onto a flagstone pavement, backing into the
sea on one side and the slope of the hill on the other. In
summer it is paradise, but in winter the cold blows down
the closes and the harbour swell beats at the back windows
of the houses and threatens to spill up over the slipways.
There are no front gardens here. Doors lead straight from
the street into living rooms and warm kitchens, and people
appear and disappear from one to another like actors entering
stage left and exiting stage right.

The doors are often open – burglary in Orkney won't get
you further than the queue for the ferry. I message a local

teacher I know from Edinburgh to ask if he's about for a pint. He says he's busy rehearsing for a Christmas show, but that I can go and keep warm at his place off the back of the water, a harbour loft converted into a warm open-plan home with views across the sound to the sea cliffs in Hoy. The door's unlocked and there's coffee in the cupboard, which is gold in this weather. I make myself comfortable on the sofa, slip off my wet shoes and socks and leave them by the radiator, and start marking some exam papers while I wait for the day to tick over. As I sit, the replies ping into my email. Hastily requested interviews are confirmed or politely declined. I think Orkney must be the most polite place in Scotland.

'You're less annoying than I thought you'd be', Rhona says when I introduce myself in the atrium of the building where we've agreed to meet. She has a point – Orkney's role as one of the world's leading sites for marine renewable energy has also made it a Mecca for people seeking information, breezing through to go back to their universities and newsrooms to talk about the brave little islands at the top of Scotland. People who work with energy in Orkney get a new request for interviews every week, and it becomes self-reinforcing. The more people hear about the Orkney energy miracle, the more people want to come and see the future being made. If Scotland is a laboratory for the future then Orkney is a great specimen, but people are not lab rats and the Orcadians do not always wish to be bottled, stamped and filed for the benefit of others. There is a pre-packaged narrative about Orkney's green revolution and a more complex one.

Fuel poverty is still a major problem – stories circulate of the old freezing in their homes, unable to pay the electricity prices set by the mainland energy companies even as Scotland creates more green power than it could ever need, and of locals forced out of the housing market by second-homers and low wages. Despite the gas fields due east of the islands, people never gained access to central heating, relying on stoves and expensive electric ranges. The houses are poorly insulated, leaking heat and money.

Rhona knits and we chat. She waves to people as they come through the main doors and make for the traybakes and scones on the table next to us. I am introduced to multiple faces I cannot remember the names of.

She explains the complexities of the situation – Orkney is a place where people jump from job to job, but where your boss is also your neighbour and your neighbour is also your doctor or your child's teacher. It creates a particular dynamic and you can't just wade in and steamroller the local population in the way energy companies are used to. In Stromness the energy revolution has been well received, but it has also changed the town. Even more so, for all the outward-facing research and development, the international awards and the technology grants from the south, it doesn't always translate into better lives for the people living in the shadow of the race for clean energy.

The cakes are laid out for a community information event, to make local people feel heard in the rush to a zero-carbon economy. I file into the hall together with the Orcadian public to listen to speakers from all over the islands and beyond. The government in Edinburgh has declared Orkney, Shetland and the Outer Hebrides key sites in the race to zero carbon, and this is an example of the social hanging onto the coat-tails of the technological. Some of the questions are prosaic – will this create jobs? Who is going to benefit if this goes ahead? Others cover the technical specifics of electric planes and wind income. In a world of eight billion, Orkney's twenty-two thousand islanders are grains of sand in the eye of the energy monster, but this is also a site of genuine transformation.

In the coffee break I'm approached by an enthusiastic American woman who looks for my name badge to try and place me. When she can't find one she asks who I am. She's spotted the radio microphone in my hand and the earphone dangling from my jacket pocket next to the bulging and now damp notebook of field notes.

I explain I'm an opportunistic interloper, hiding from the storm, and flash my university ID card. The picture looks nothing like me – taken when I was still seriously ill, with tired eyes and no colour in my face – but there's a flicker of recognition at the name. Usually people say, 'I've seen your byline' or 'I recognise you from the radio.' It's hard to know if they're being polite or whether they're confusing me with someone else. The brain has a remarkable ability to build false memories to fill the gaps.

Realising she's speaking to a fellow traveller she moves into a less formal mode and introduces herself as Susan, a Professor of Transition Engineering employed at one of the big universities back in the central belt. She has a smooth southern drawl a world away from the precise consonants of Orcadian English, tempered slightly by the years in international academia.

Susan runs a transition-engineering laboratory in a building down the hill, drawn to Orkney by energy research and what she calls Orcadian 'knackie-handedness', the ability to try out and innovate with what you have in front of you. Flanked by her German PhD students, she reels off the achievements and problems. The race to decarbonise is like the space programme, but getting two people to the surface of the moon is easier than weaning eight billion off carbon in the space of twenty years.

Engineers and scientists are not just machines in the service of technological development. Engineering research gets more money than social science because politicians think it's the engine of the economy, but social science graduates are as employable as engineers and computer scientists. When it comes to stopping climate change, the solution is not just more investment in technology, but about transforming the relationship between people, energy and social life.

'Twenty years ago my son asked me, "Well, Mom, are those things gonna work?"' Susan says as we sit on a bench by a poster display about high-capacity battery storage. 'I said that even if everyone like me was successful that wouldn't change what it is that's causing the risks.' I nod, thinking about Dounreay and the belief of the nuclear pioneers that reactor technology would do what renewables are now promising. 'My son decided for me', she tells me. 'He said: "Mom, you have to figure out what we need to do and how to do it".'

Electrification is the best weapon we have against climate change, clean at the point of use and clean at the point of creation with the political will. Renewables are almost infinitely scalable, and when they get going renewable electricity is cheap, but it needs social adaptation as well as technology. Renewables cannot absolve us of the deeper sins of the oil age, guilt-free plastic consumerism and mobility and endless growth.

We live on the cusp of a world where energy is clean, cheap and decentralised, but it will look very different to how we think of energy now. For over a century the orthodox view was that there should be large-scale power stations to meet the energy needs of developed and developing countries, run by big private companies or the state, but this no longer holds true. Orkney is one massive, distributed generation field, turning out more energy than it could ever use domestically but struggling for things to do with it because of a lack of imagination from the rest of the country.

Susan originally trained as a mechanical engineer. She deals fundamentally in the slow facts of research and development. They jar with the promises and hype of green technologists hunting for funding and investment. 'We need to be as honest about energy technology as we are about how gears work', she says. When I listen back to the recording later I scroll through the file several times on my laptop to take in the full force of one particular passage.

'Stories are worth a lot of money ... I'm not sure our story has really evolved to that point, even if our research has. The narratives of exploring new technologies are perhaps stronger than the narratives of exploring how to live with the resources that you have.'

Orkney is lucky in that it has almost boundless renewable resources, and its future is unambiguously electric, yet some parts of the electric dream are more realistic than others. There are home batteries going into public housing, and a new offshore wind farm part-owned by the islands themselves is going into the water off the west side. It will do what was denied to Shetland, taking the energy of the Atlantic storm fronts and turning it into money to pay for roads and piers, houses and schools.

The other word on people's lips in Stromness is hydrogen. Even before the Berlin Wall came down, much of Europe came to rely on cheap gas from Eastern Europe and the North Sea, and while it is not a direct replacement, hydrogen can run district heating, cargo ships and heavy machinery, as well as emergency power stations if the renewable grid fails. Making hydrogen from wind just to burn it for heat is hugely inefficient when compared to running an electric heater, but hydrogen can be stored and used when the wind stops blowing and manufactured using excess energy that would otherwise go to waste. People in Orkney and Shetland are beginning to talk about becoming hydrogen exporters, selling to Germany and the Netherlands where tens of millions of people are in desperate need of clean heat. The oil terminal in the island of Flotta across from Stromness has plans for a new hydrogen plant using the offshore wind farms to create combustible zero-carbon fuel. Suddenly Orkney looks far more modern than the creaking cities of the mainland.

I make for the Flattie, the Stromness bar named after the local flat-bottomed rowing boats that used to fill the harbours of Stromness and Kirkwall. It's closed, boarded up since I was last through, as is the hotel upstairs. I'd been hoping for a few hours by the open coal fire before my next interview and the storm has got worse, so I do a circle of the alternatives, passing the darkened library and the tourist shops until I settle on the one open café. On the shorefront is a store called 'Leviathan International'. I wonder whether the owners are familiar with how multinational energy companies behave.

In the café the hours are drawn out over mugs of hot tea and chips with grated cheese on top, watching the clock tick down. Outside the window the ferry to the mainland is confined to port by the weather, rocking at her moorings, the name *MV Hamnavoe* picked out by the spotlights of the passenger terminal.

To grasp the power of the water around Orkney the best thing to do is to stand on the deck of the *Hamnavoe* when conditions are only just safe to sail. The Pentland Firth between Orkney and Caithness is less than ten miles across at its narrowest point and twice a day the water is squeezed through it as the North Sea and the Atlantic meet. It has one of the strongest tidal surges on earth. The passage is dangerous, and ships still regularly run into trouble when conditions are particularly bad. A few years back eight people died when their bulk cargo freighter started taking on water and sank on its way from Denmark to the Irish Sea.

The *Hamnavoe* is built like a tank and is powerful enough to push through the worst currents, but even so, when the sea swell is high docking can be impossible. On the worst crossings the tell-tale change in pitch as the propellers come out of the water is met ten seconds later by the prow rising on the waves and the crash as the stern goes back in. Even on a good day tourists stumble across the helicopter deck trying to take photos as the boat pitches under the sea cliffs of Hoy. Someone I know in Kirkwall once spent twenty hours on the ferry, stuck in a no man's land between Scotland and Stromness waiting for the weather to change.

In the Pentland Firth the sea seems to flow uphill, the marine equivalent of what in Scotland is known as an electric brae, a road that looks to slope in one direction but pulls you in the other. The tidal races of the firth are a goldmine for marine power because tides are predictable, providing guaranteed yields year-round and regular and reliable grid loadings.

Rich the teacher has texted me again to say he's just remembered someone I should speak to, an engineer working on experimental wave power who is in port due to the weather. I get another email telling me someone I was supposed to meet can't make it because of a sick child who needs taking to the doctor in Kirkwall, so I text the number Rich has given me and get a reply. We go back and forth, ruling out places to meet that are either closed or closing, and settle on Stromness's go-to pub, the Ferry Inn.

The Ferry is all varnished wood and cushioned corners like the inside of a 1950s coal steamer. If this were anywhere else it would be a too on-the-nose theme bar, the walls adorned with marine charts and paraphernalia. The faces in the Ferry are mostly local – there are very few tourists in mid-December – but in Orkney local is not a watertight concept. Stromness is a global village: Germans, Norwegians, Spaniards, South Americans, Dutch, Americans and Japanese. I'm there to meet an Argentinian.

'If the weather is good you can go outside, and when it isn't you don't need the window', says Diego with a chuckle when I ask him about the lack of glazing in the pub. He pitched up in Orkney when at college and stayed, graduating to work for one of the local offshore companies on the boats that deploy experimental wave tech in the strong tidal reaches. It's so loud I don't even bother turning on the recorder, scribbling in my bad handwriting in the notebook instead.

Diego is an engineer by training, working with the offshore crews to deploy underwater turbines and get them in and out of the water for repair and maintenance. Some of it has never been done before, and computer models only tell you so much in advance. 'Sometimes you make something, it breaks and then you have to go back and make it again, better,' he laughs, 'and you have to go back to the person paying you and explain that this thing you made for them has broken and it will be weeks or months before they can do it again.'

The difference between building a wind turbine on land and sticking it under the sea is as big as the difference between a jumbo jet and a space shuttle. Electric turbines made of metal don't like salt water; the internal components have to be kept dry and the outside has to cope with immersion in the sea for months at a time. Barnacles latch on to the metalwork, anchors come loose and debris shifts across the seabed, battering the blades. Some of the turbines that show their faces on the dockside after immersion look like relics of a lost civilisation.

Marine energy is a world of trial and error, with companies permanently on the hunt for new investment to chase the prize of successful, large-scale and limitless tidal and wave power. Oceans make up 71 per cent of the world's surface, all moving with the sun and moon and the circulating heat of the ocean currents. The race for reliable and scalable marine energy outstrips even wind in potential. The pace of progress has been phenomenal, but energy investors are still reluctant to pump in money without guarantees of return. Whoever holds the patents on the successful designs and is willing to bear the risk will have a licence to print money, and could yet save the world at the same time.

On a climate-changed planet, conserving and using energy efficiently is as important as how it is generated. If local turbines are a licence to print money, ineffective use of electricity is like burning rolled up fifty-pound notes. Every joule that seeps out of old windows and thin walls could be doing work somewhere else, running ferries or hospital ventilators, charging electric arc furnaces, or keeping the lights on in commercial greenhouses in the winter darkness. Heat, food, movement and life all flow from electricity in the north.

I'm fading and turn down the offer of another beer; I need to drive even if the roads are empty. The car's waiting and I want my bed and the hotel and the guilty relief of chemically-aided sleep. Mindful of the need to do everything properly even as the fatigue hits, I hand Diego the crumpled side of A4 from my bag with the project information and permission sheet. He reads through it methodically.

'Very interesting. Have you spoken to Lara?'

Lara turns out to be a Spanish anthropologist who is hiding from the storm with the flu, heaters on to keep a small Orcadian house hospitable. She apologises for not being able to come out but promises to speak to me once things improve, and I head back to Kirkwall in the car to a warm bed and twenty pages of fresh notes. The weather report shows the storm is moving northwards and the ferry will be going again soon, but it's still punishingly cold and my skin craves natural light. Across Scapa Flow I can see the dock lights on Hoy and Flotta clearly, driving the long way round on the high road to see if there are any oil platforms moored up behind the safety of the causeways. Through the murk the tell-tale shape of a rig is visible in the rain, moored in the shallows of the voe.

There are plenty of studies of the nuts and bolts of renewable energy, armies of social scientists carrying out community-impact studies and economic analysis, filing reports that are read by civil servants and condensed into a page of briefing for government ministers. Growth potential, economic opportunity, capital investment and carbon targets are the basic code that writes the future in the world of energy policy, but Lara does something different. When we meet in a café she's recovered and I'm beginning to feel better.

She's interested in how energy creates different forms of social life, of how, freed from the dead weight of oil, we might build new societies just as oil built a new world in its image. Energy makes life, and electricity can make different kinds of life altogether.

'I study the justice implications of emerging energy technologies', she says succinctly in a Spanish accent, more heavily inflected with mid-Atlantic drift on the sound file than I remember from the interview itself. The harms of any energy project are spread over time and space, and her work is focused on how things can be done in a way that benefits the majority, recognising the intrinsic worth and dignity of people, of nature and of the future generations who cannot yet speak, but who have already had their world upended by climate change.

She takes issue with the idea of Orkney as a living laboratory for the future. Like Rhona had told me over the sound of her knitting needles, the idea of Orkney as a test centre that can solve the world's problems is no better than the idea of the north coast as a pristine wilderness that can heal people through the power of nature. It robs people of autonomy in the story being told, making them avatars in a simulation to be run and re-run for the benefit of others.

We go back to basics and talk shop over coffee, about energy anthropology and the fallibility of climate dreams, a reminder of the fact that academia can still spark the synapses into life when it's unencumbered by micromanagement and the changing whims of funders and politicians. Sometimes all you need to do is get in the car and go and have a look.

We talk for too long; the recording stops but we carry on chatting until the clock beats us. 'But', she finishes optimistically, 'we have a genuine transformational opportunity to reimagine what our societies look like.'

Eventually she has to run to take one of the planes that shuttles back and forth between Orkney and urban Scotland, for now at least still running on fossil fuel. Even as we make the future we do so with the tools of the present, entangled with technology that feels more and more anachronistic the longer we stare at it.

I sit on the pier waiting for the hand signal to roll onto the boat. The weather is still foul and I know the crossing will be unpleasant, but I have the heater running again and *Good*

Morning Scotland on, listening to the BBC weather reports from the studio by the Clyde in Glasgow. When I come to start the engine, nothing happens. The car is dead. Even petrol needs electricity to work. It makes sense to cut out the middleman.

Two of the shore crew appear with a battery pack and flip up the bonnet, gesturing for me to turn the key. The battery sparks and the petroleum fumes ignite obediently. The headlights come on again and they pull back, snapping the latch closed and patting it to make sure the spring has been pinned down before retreating to the safety of the mess room. Dawn comes as we sail out into the open sea, under the cliffs of Hoy and towards home.

The boat comes into port on the mainland and Dounreay looms in the half-light further east. The power lines that used to carry nuclear energy now carry the collective might of the Caithness windfields and the Orkney arrays. Among the horror of climate change this feels fundamentally like a wellspring of real hope, where transformation is genuinely possible.

In the grey morning I follow the power lines south again until mountains become fields and fields become towns, suburbs and cities, back home to the Scotland of motorways and traffic jams and millions of people squeezed into a narrow strip of permanently lit tarmac. I hit the Cromarty Firth and take the direct route over the bridge to Inverness, skipping the back road to Dingwall and Seóras in his pyjamas, a dot on a car GPS moving through an electric landscape, moving on.

7

Unweather and uveðr

The sea is rippled but unbreaking, the first day in weeks for a clear sailing as the ferry bobs on the Atlantic swell. It judders as it hauls itself out of Oban harbour and past the lighthouse at the far end of Lismore, west towards the open ocean beyond the Inner Hebrides. The usual boat is broken and the emergency standby is past retirement, lines of rust running down her bows where water has channelled through the hawseholes. The plastic flooring peels upwards where it meets the wall, but the cosmetic damage is not worth fixing. Just months later she is due to be put into storage and unceremoniously stripped for parts in what remains of the Glasgow shipyards.

The *MV Hebridean Isles* has a Gaelic name too, *Eileanan Innse Gall* – the Gaelic Islands, which tourists clumsily mispronounce and Scots don't do much better at. Scots and Gaels are not one and the same and it's a big step from the people who like to toast their New Year suppers in Gaelic to the people who live and breathe the language in daily life. Over the tannoy come the familiar bilingual announcements welcoming the passengers on board. '*Tha an sgiobar agus an sgioba a' cur Fàilte oirrbh air bòrd...*' You can tell the age of the boat from the side-loading ramps that stick up from her open deck, a reminder of the time when many of the islands lacked proper piers and the boats would come at the slipways side-on. As I set myself up in the lounge for the eight-hour crossing and bed down on the benches, I see an emergency mechanic welcomed on board and shown to his cabin. With no other boats available the power unit has to survive a few months more.

An hour later he re-emerges into the cafeteria and starts streaming films on his phone to ward off the boredom. At the table behind I join a video call with the support group my doctor has sent me to once a week, where people with neurological issues talk about their experiences. Some of us have been in road accidents, some have had long COVID, and some have had strokes or aneurysms. The common thread is trying to make sense of life afterwards. We could all do with a dedicated mechanic to keep us going.

The call ends and we say our goodbyes. I'll never meet these people in real life but we know more about one another's illnesses than even my family know about mine. I close the laptop and step out onto the deck. The sun has begun to move down towards the south and the rays stream up from Ireland to soak the Hebrides in solar radiation for the final half-hour of the day. The boat is half-empty, just me, the mechanic and some crofters taking empty trailers back to Lochboisdale in South Uist. I was five years old when I sailed this way for the first time, out through the Sound of Mull and into the swell of the Atlantic towards Barra and Uist in a boat that seemed like a cathedral. Thirty years later I can walk the length of it in the space of a minute.

I settle out of the wind under the bridge. The older boats have a public foredeck that has been replaced by watertight viewing windows on the new vessels, and something has been lost with it. A pod of dolphins appears and dances briefly across the bow. In every direction there is golden light. I count the hills: Skye, Uist, Barra and the high peaks of Lochaber with white on their summits. For a moment the boat hangs equidistant from each of them as if strung on four threads from the mountaintops. Grey pillars of snow dip down to touch the sea before moving on.

The crossing to the Western Isles can be thrilling or deeply unpleasant, depending on your disposition. A few years before I'd injured myself in a fall on my way over on a lifeline sailing, when the government-run ferries make the crossing in bad weather to keep the islands connected through the winter storms. The boat was packed with shop supplies and people trying to get home, medicine for the island pharmacies and exiles making an annual pilgrimage back to see family. The bow rose and then dropped away so suddenly that I was flung into the ceiling and then unceremoniously hammered back onto the floor in a stairwell. I couldn't walk right for a week. You have to learn to move with, not against the boat in that kind of weather.

On the calm days like today when the beaches of the Outer Hebrides are bathed in golden afternoon light and the water sits placidly, they seem like paradise. I once showed a friend from Brazil a picture of the beaches in the west I had taken on my camera phone and she refused to believe the colours could be real, birch-white sands and water so clear you can stand up to your shoulders and see your feet. It's only the temperature and the threat of snow on the breeze that reminds you this is early spring in the North Atlantic.

The low-lying shores of Uist are a muted green for much of the year, peppered with crofts where the smallholders have carefully cultivated the lands between the hills and the sea.

This ecosystem co-produced by people, animals and the sea – the machair – provides fertile soil but also a bulwark against the ocean itself. Just a few feet above water level, the crofts of Western Uist are at the front line of the battle with the Atlantic ocean.

The Hebrides were made by the sea, culturally and geographically. Machair sand, that forms the basis of the field systems, is made up of biocarbonate material from pulverised seashells as well as post-glacial debris, and the alkaline machair is influenced by the calcium of the shells. Traditionally crofters would fertilise the ground with seaweed, leading to a unique form of agriculture that engineered the land for crops but also changed it to form a bulwark behind the constantly shifting and fragile dune system in a fragile interplay with the water and weather.

Uist is made up of three main islands – North Uist, Benbecula and South Uist, linked by causeways made of rock sunk into the sandy tidal races and salt marsh between them. When there is a perfect storm of tides, winds and rainwater the narrow passages between the islands are subject to violent surges as water is pushed in from the open Atlantic, with strong undertows in the channels and around the reefs. Before the causeways the islands were reliant on expert skippers navigating the rocks and sandbars in small boats, or a long trip in one of the mainland ferries circling far out to sea through the deeper channels.

It's pushing towards midnight when we get to Lochboisdale. The ferry dispenses its sheep trailers and pickups onto dry land and I power the car up through the night, counting the miles across South Uist as the damp asphalt rolls under the wheels and guides me across the causeways to Benbecula in the black. Now and then a pair of lights swings in from a side track or a lit window forms a square of warmth on the charcoal canvas, but otherwise I am alone in the February darkness.

When I wake in Benbecula the sun rises behind new snow clouds and the water froths pebble-grey where it meets the wide beaches on the island's western side. I've an appointment at the local government buildings by the airport, so I pour my coffee into a travel cup and slot it into the plastic cavity by the car handbrake.

Balivanich, the village where the airport and council offices lie, grew up around a military airfield that found new life as a test range for rockets, and though the military presence is much diminished the place still feels more like an air-force outpost than an organic settlement. Benbecula's architecture is best described as utilitarian. Modernisation came at a time when concrete and pebbledash were yet to give way to the big Nordic windows and wooden panels in the semiotic of architectural progress.

The offices of the *Comhairle Nan Eilean Siar* are no different, a long bungalow facing onto a windy car park by the island cash machine. The *Comhairle* is unlike any other local council in Scotland. The only place in the country where government takes place bilingually, politicians flip back and forth between English and Gaelic, as do much of the population. Travelling in the west is always a firm reminder that there is England, and there is Britain, and that they're not the same.

Úisdean is waiting for me in a side room, sitting behind a desk with a broken top that rattles when I put the bag down on it and pull out my equipment. None of the public buildings in Scotland are in very good shape, it seems, the refurbishments deferred just like the ferry maintenance to save money as austerity bites. Úisdean's gloves are resting on a chair, but he keeps his hat and coat on, looking like a man just on his way out. I know people in the Hebrides who live in boiler suits and outdoor jackets six days a week, zipped up against the weather as they move from car to field to home and back again.

Úisdean is a politician without a party, like Mick in his miners' club with his Labour membership card consigned to history. Unlike Mick, Úisdean never had one; party politics is not big in the Hebrides – the machines in London and Edinburgh have little impact out here and his political education was working to fix drains and roads up and down the islands, alongside managing his family croft. Politics here isn't without disagreement, but Uist and the rest of the Hebrides are communitarian by necessity. The ferries, the roads and the airports are common to everyone, as is the weather.

Someone up in Stornoway in Lewis had put me in touch with Úisdean when I asked about climate change. He chairs the *Comhairle*'s infrastructure committee and sees all the challenges facing the Hebrides on a daily basis. He is also, in the words of the *Leosiach* contact who first gave me his name, 'a well-connected gentleman'.

'You want to highlight the difficulties but you don't want to overdo it at the same time; it gives a negative impression of the place and we have a wonderful way of life', Úisdean reflects in the light Uist English dialect. People who don't know the Western Isles accent can hear it the first time and think they're speaking to a German or Scandinavian. To listen to Gaelic as an English speaker is a dislocating experience as people reveal whole new sides of themselves, jumping from one language to another without changes in the tone or pace, mixing liberally. Gaels can be Scots but most Scots will never be Gaels.

Úisdean is the latest of a generation of smallholders running a few fields and some livestock, usually around their day jobs. There are not really farms in the conventional sense in the islands, and not a lot of profit to be made from agriculture, but crofting is more central to the sociology of the west than it is to anywhere else in Scotland.

'My father assigned me the croft when I was twenty-one', says Úisdean, staring at a space over my shoulder where he visualises the memory. 'I loved crofting', he adds half-wistfully. 'I didn't make money out of it, for sure, but I thoroughly enjoy it. It clears the mind from a hard day at work and it's a decent way of life.'

Úisdean is a heavily studied man. Like in Orkney, geography field trips, newspaper journalists, government researchers and anthropologists from North American universities all pass through wanting to hear his accounts of daily life in the islands. Some want to document birds and whales, some want to study the *Uibhisteachs* themselves, and some want to write about the vanishing land. They come armed with expensive cameras, microphones and permission forms, seeking out places and people that allow them to go back to their paymasters with hard data. Like Rhona in Stromness, Úisdean casts one eye over the permission forms and notes drily that I'm not the first person to sit there with a list of questions and my stack of ethical paperwork.

The serenity of the office is interrupted every so often by the drone of turboprops landing at the airport across the road. They come through far more clearly on the microphone than the human ear picks up. Úisdean is just back from a trip off-island. 'Yesterday I came over Benbecula in the plane and all you could see there was fields underwater', he says as the noise of the engines subsides.

Uist has a few small hills, but the majority of the population live in townships on the flat land around the coast. The causeways that were built to connect the islands have changed the currents, which has meant sand ripped from one place and dumped in another as the coastline constantly shifts, leaving the land behind the beaches exposed. Even without rising sea levels the Atlantic is slowly eating the islands, but climate change is making it far worse.

'You keep just moving back; even in my own village where the land is rocky the fence keeps moving back', says Úisdean, gesturing on an imaginary map in mid-air towards his family holding just off the road north. 'But if you really want to see the problems you should go to Baleshare.'

Baleshare is a small tidal island off the western side of North Uist accessed by another stone causeway. Completely flat and at no point higher than twelve metres above sea level, the western side of the island is slowly being gouged away by the Atlantic waves. The eastern side is regularly overwhelmed by storm surges that push up the tidal races, dragging the shoreline back into the sea as they recede.

Úisdean gives me some directions and some names and I leave him to attend to his council business. I get a message back as the car is buffeted by the wind in the car park and start the engine, heading up the main road from Benbecula across the tidal races, before turning off the main and making over the dunes to the shore, swinging round a 90-degree bend and onto the causeway to Baleshare. I'm in luck – just a few days before it was impassable. The community social-media pages share the regular coastguard warnings of the tidal surges. Residents can be trapped on or off the island for a few days at a time when the weather turns.

The wind is severe, straight from the north-west and strong enough that it takes a few attempts to open the door. Cars in Uist are not just a means of transport but mobile shelters. It isn't unusual to see people parked up sipping coffee in the front seat at the beach or tourists driven from their expensively purchased tents asleep in the back when a storm comes in. From a side track another car appears and Morag, the tenant of one of the crofts overlooking the causeway, beckons me over to the leeward side. She was the one who sent me the message and asks me if I want to go somewhere less windy to chat, but there isn't really anywhere else to go.

She works for the National Health Service and travels all over the Outer Hebrides, but the family are Baleshare natives. As the tidal surges overwhelm the ageing and increasingly threadbare road, she's started a campaign to highlight the island's plight.

Morag points back up the gravel track to where the family home perches on the ness, the small promontory stretching out towards the tidal sands.

'We lost two sheep to the sea there in the last storms when the water came up', she says. 'You wouldn't believe it now but it was almost at the house. It seems unbelievable at low water – the house is a good eight feet above the beach and much higher than the road.'

Whenever the island is cut off, life is thrown into chaos. It wasn't climate change that built the Baleshare causeway too low and without enough stormwater culverts, but it isn't helping. It's notoriously difficult to link individual storms to climate change, but extreme weather events are shifting from once a century to around once a decade or more. At best it will make life difficult; at worst, large parts of the Atlantic rim will become uninhabitable as infrastructure is repeatedly battered by the fluctuating weather and rising sea levels.

In 2005, a storm hit Uist that decimated the exposed western side of the archipelago and led to the death of a family trying to flee the coastal surges. As their convoy of cars made its way from South Uist to Benbecula over the fixed links they were swept off the road and into the sea. It was a very public tragedy. Two children and three adults were killed that night in the winter darkness. In a community as tight-knit as Uist the loss lay heavy long afterwards.

The single-track ribbon of road that threads its way up the west side of the archipelago links clusters of houses together, gravel tracks falling away towards the beach where the dunes shift on an almost weekly basis. Exactly how much sea levels rise in the next century depends on a number of factors, but if the Greenland ice sheet continues to disintegrate it will raise the Atlantic by up to a metre. The shallow channels between the islands will expand as the coastlines of the lowest-lying islands shrink or are subsumed almost altogether. Uist's long sandy beaches will be eroded into the sea and the dunes behind them will be broken into new beaches, while the farmland behind the dunes will turn into tidal bog. The airport is almost at sea level, and the runway has already been reinforced. It will simply not be practical to save some areas.

Morag starts her engine and hurries off to work over the causeway, while I drive over to the seaward side of Baleshare, where the beach is so eroded I almost take the car straight off the end of the track and onto the sand five feet below. Here the shoreline is littered with material gouged from the back of the beach, mixing with driftwood and bits of plastic thrown ashore on the waves. Where the beach begins to undercut the farmland the island is visible in cross-section, crumbling strata of sand and gravel with nothing to protect it. The beach already feels like the scene of a lost battle.

* * *

It's summer when I come back to the Outer Hebrides. The *Loch Portain*, the little car ferry that treks back and forth between Uist and the Isle of Harris, is specially built to operate in the tidal races. It picks its way through the skerries on a zigzag route to avoid the worst of the reefs, and as I roll the car down the slipway and onto the ridged deck the weather clears to give views across the whole expanse of water. Even with good skippering the ferry has made contact with the seabed – as the ferry company euphemistically describe it – on multiple occasions. Gazing down over the side, the sandy bottom is easy to see in the crystal water. Fish dart away from the noise of the propellers, and in the distance the hills of Harris grow larger. When Stanley Kubrick needed to show the surface of an alien world to go alongside his spherical spaceships he flew a plane over the mountains of North Harris, inverting the colours to make the black streams and lochs glow bright orange like lava flows and molten pools. Kubrick couldn't have known, but the Lewisian gneiss that runs through the landscape would have looked that way two and a half billion years ago, bubbling and folding under unimaginable pressure on a younger earth yet to give rise to complex life.

I'm going up to one of the most exposed places in Scotland, Gallan Head, on the western tip of Lewis at the top of the archipelago. The spring snows are gone and it is light pretty much all the time, bar a few muted hours of half-dark in the early morning. I've agreed to swap Glasgow for a few weeks croft-sitting looking after an errant sheepdog in an abandoned military barracks on a clifftop, tending the chickens and ducks in the garden and feeding the sheep for some friends who have gone south.

Gallan Head and the neighbouring village of Aird Uig are curiosities. The whole headland and village were closed and militarised for much of the cold war when the promontory was home to a radar base like the one at Saxa Vord in Shetland, and if the rumours are true, a UK government bio-warfare research station. When the military eventually moved on it became a destination for people who wanted to live cheaply a long way from anywhere. The landscape around is dotted with guardhouses and abandoned outbuildings, left to decay in the weather.

From Gallan Head there's a clear line of sight to the horizon, broken only by tankers and cruise ships and the sea cliffs of the St Kilda archipelago that fade in and out of view as the mist rolls across the water. St Kilda is the island that didn't make it through, abandoned by its population in 1930, never to return. Many of the St Kildans ended up in Glasgow, where the remnants of their unique Gaelic-speaking culture were subsumed into industrial urban life.

I'm nominally in Lewis to recover – I've been knocked out again by fatigue and dizziness – and a few weeks in the islands is far from work. The dog keeps me from looking at my computer and is a good excuse to take the paths over the headland and down to the small beaches on either side. You can train other breeds to work as sheepdogs, but Scottish collies are superior, save the madness. The breed is an unpredictable combination of loyal intelligence and borderline insanity, and Ziggy is very much at the wild-card end.

Out the back of the house is the enclosure where the ducks and chickens live. Eggs from both hatch around the same time but each day makes it clearer that they are different beasts. The ducklings are already bigger and more headstrong, nipping at my fingers when I stick my hand into the coop. One night I manage to get them into an ice-cream tub and into the bathroom for their first-ever swim. The dog scratches at the door but we ignore him. They lose their fear of me as I run a finger across the back of their heads and slowly open the tap until they can half-swim in the inch of water. I cup them in my hands to put them in, dipping my finger to make sure it isn't too hot.

Instinctively they whip the droplets into the air with their beaks and quack contentedly as they circle around the tub. Freed from the coop and the company of the chickens, they have begun to live in a slightly larger world. I lie back, with my head resting on the wall of the tiny bathroom and my feet up on the closed toilet seat, sipping black tea while the dog sits indignantly in the hallway listening to the quacks. He's stopped scratching, but when I open the door his black nose immediately posts itself through the crack. He can tell we're having fun.

Ziggy is harmless but has a pathological desire to chase and catch anything with feathers. Out on a walk up past the ruins of the military radar station he picks up terrified tern chicks from their burrows on the ground and shows them to me. They have to be gently removed from his jaws and put back, unhurt but traumatised. He seems pleased with himself and can't work out why I'm not more impressed.

England has been baking in a record heatwave, but Lewis is shrouded in mist and buffeted by storms coming off the warm sea. On midsummer the sun never breaks through and the ragtag bunch of hippies and campervanners who have trekked north to welcome it are met by a damp wall of Atlantic air. Aird is just west of Callanish, the stone circle built five thousand years ago by a pre-Celtic culture. Lewis has been a centre of Iron Age, Norse and Celtic civilisation and Callanish serves as a reminder both of what endures and what doesn't. The concrete of Aird Uig's low military buildings won't last as long as the stones around the coast, but the radar base's reinforced slabs and breeze-blocks will become artefacts all the same, records of the decades before the climate changed and eclipsed Soviet or Russian attack as the biggest threat to global stability.

Ziggy and I continue our walk and pass an abandoned sentry house that has become a sheepfold, drowning in mud and the unmistakable smell of sheep shit. From the ruin a man emerges, dressed in a boiler suit and wellies. He uses his body to shield newly rolled cigarettes from the wind, a pick-me-up as the longest days drift on into half-night. Long wisps of grey hair in what was once a thick ponytail dance on the wind. I've hardly slept in the constant twilight and it's near eight but as bright as in the early afternoon. The dog eyes are the same pearl blue as the half light off the sea.

Brian is the last large-scale crofter in Aird, farming full time. He recognises the dog and I tell him I'm looking after the house and croft. I try and make conversation about the storm due in a few days, but he brushes it off. This one looks like it will be insignificant, he says.

'When you've lived here your experience of what a storm is changes', he tells me between puffs. 'We've had storms here that have taken water right up over the headland and down the other side and taken the roofs off the buildings.' I look back down to Gallan Head where the land narrows, imagining the sea spray arcing over from one side to the other. The cliffs are a hundred feet high.

Brian is an incomer too – he moved up to escape the deprivation and industrial decline of 1980s Newcastle and stayed, but still laments the tailing off of crofting as a way of life. People don't like getting up at the crack of dawn or heading out to fetch stray sheep in the winter darkness if they can help it, and there's little money to be had. Crofting today, more than ever before, is about balancing jobs and government subsidies, and about calling in favours from the local community. Brian used to drive the local minibus until the funding ran out. The price of diesel has skyrocketed due to the energy crisis. His jeep and tractor are now left at home if he can.

A thousand years ago the islands were part of the Viking Kingdom of the Isles that stretched from Norway to Ireland, the crossroads trade in a maritime state. Many of the place names are Norse, rendered in the Gaelic that replaced it that has in turn been put under existential threat from English. The Vikings who colonised the Hebrides had a world-view shaped by their experience of the sea. In Old Norse there's a word for weather, but also for 'unweather', *úveðr*, when the conditions flip and the world around becomes difficult to negotiate. Climate change does not just mean more bad weather, but unweather. It's an upending of everything we have come to know.

Brian has just been chasing a missing sheep, which he's still not found. Losses are nothing unusual when animals graze freely, but in the storms sheep looking for shelter often fall down the steep clefts in the coastline or get trapped out in the weather. The following morning I will find it dead on the beach with its eyes already taken by the birds.

The conversation fades as the wind increases and Brian's roll-up burns to its natural end. I steer Ziggy on and down to the cliff edge. We sit staring into the swell and out towards St Kilda to the south-west as the clock pushes towards midnight, me and the dog and the Atlantic rising and turning at our feet.

'If you're in the West, make sure you speak to Padraig', I'd been told by another exiled *Uibhisteach* living in Glasgow.

The reason why is clear as soon as I meet him in an old church in Grimsay, the small flat island tucked under the eastern flank of North Uist known for its commanding views and sheltered harbour. After missing him the first time I'm back on my way through Lewis to the mainland. Padraig is only in his twenties but has the bearing of an older soul, and he knows Grimsay with the knowledge of generations.

The Church is a fading institution across Scotland, but in the west faith is still strong. Padraig is the son of a minister, a crofter on the island, a musician, a Gaelic intellectual and much else besides. He has just finished a new project called *Túsanaich*, Gaelic for indigenous, about the connection between the language and the environment. We chat about mutual friends and common interests while we wait for our coffee.

'The wider point of identity is definitely very strong', he says over the table in the corner of the church café. He has a PhD in music based on his Gaelic compositions and is up front about the politics behind the slow death of the language. He talks about what linguists call a post-vernacular community, where the language and customs survive but are robbed of their place in everyday life. 'The language has been lost, and for the Gaels and the Highlands and Islands the language has been lost because it was forced out.'

Úisdean had told me a story about being sent to school on the mainland in the 1960s for an English-only education where Gaelic was forbidden in the classroom. The indigenous Celtic languages of the UK that have survived have done so only because they made it through the long period when the supremacy of English was not just assumed but actively coerced. Manx and Cornish, the two other major languages of the Celtic fringe that survived into the modern era, were not so lucky. We talk about languages dying out as if it were an organic tragedy, but the people who pushed Gaelic to the brink of extinction knew what they were doing.

'People were belted in school for speaking the language', Padraig reminds me. 'Those scars run quite deep.'

The Western Isles, like Shetland and Orkney, have their own intelligentsia, people who go away to Edinburgh and Glasgow or further afield but come back. Scotland's latest national poet – appointed by the government to promote the art form – comes from Ness at the top of the archipelago, a big symbolic win for the language on the international stage. As one of Scotland's sixty thousand native Gaelic speakers, Padraig is as immersed in the language as it is possible to be now. Being a big fish in a small pond is scant compensation for the slow retreat of the tongue.

Outsiders have a fondness for cherry-picking the lost words of dying languages and pretending they have a unique value, relegating the Gaels to a curiosity on the European fringe. Living languages are forged by context, though, and Gaelic also has words for nuclear power station, hospital closure, climate change, decentralisation and renewable energy. Anthropologists and scholars of racism talk about the colonisation of the mind, the idea that a minority culture can internalise how the coloniser sees it. Part of the challenge is to let the language evolve among its users rather than make it a museum piece or an elegy to what has been lost.

The islands need people, but those incomers are invariably not Gaelic-speaking, so as one problem is solved another worsens. Discrimination on grounds of language is illegal, and most incomers do not arrive as children, when the brain is more plastic and languages are easier to pick up. The dream of a future Hebrides is not one of retreat and decline, but of modernisation that gives Gaelic culture its own autonomous future.

Padraig points out that for all its vulnerability, Uist is still more communitarian than places on the mainland. People help each other out with no expectation of repayment, they work together and they share burdens. It's an economy that doesn't show up on balance sheets. These are people who know how to organise even with the odds against them. In a time of global crisis that solidarity is priceless.

I drive the loop road around North Uist and back to Lochmaddy to look for the eagles that often hunt on the western flank of the island. Lochmaddy is the port village where a ferry leaves for Skye and the land fractures into long fingers and islets as it gives way to the open sea, a sheltered natural harbour with room for a whole navy.

Lochmaddy isn't big; there's a hotel, the car park at the pier and a cattle mart stretching back up the hill, and next to it a small museum and post office. The museum and gallery space, Taigh Chearsabhagh, is known for its Gaelic and environmental art. A few years ago it attracted international coverage when two Finnish artists created an installation that covered the entire bay. The concept was simple. A white band of LED lights penetrating buildings, crossing roads and ringing the hillside, showing where the high watermark will be thanks to storm surges and the predicted rise in the sea level.

If the sea level continues to rise as quickly as is currently predicted, the museum itself could be unusable in as little as twenty years. Its foundations will crumble as the ground beneath it is saturated and the wooden walls begin to rot in the sea spray. The islets that dot the approaches to Lochmaddy harbour will begin to vanish completely at high tide, just rocks marked as a hazard on marine charts.

All of this seems unreal, and yet it is borne out by the science that predicts with the utmost certainty that two degrees of global temperature rise will put half of Benbecula and much of Uist below sea level. Once you see the vulnerabilities you simply cannot unsee them.

I drive back down through Benbecula and South Uist to the ferry and the boat to the mainland, the high-water line running across the landscape in front of me all the way. It sits in a band across the back of my eyelids, a ribbon of light burned into memory.

8

Offshore

William zigzags the boat through the swell, trying to minimise the slap of the waves on the bow.

'They're just wind waves, thankfully.'

His voice is barely audible over the noise of the engines as he leans out from behind the helm. He shouts down the length of the boat to the prow where we are huddled together in our life jackets. William pushes the throttle a notch and the front of the boat rises, never having time to land before it hits the crest of the next rolling wave.

We're in a rigid inflatable (RIB) like the ones used by the lifeboat service and the Marines, two powerful engines behind the wheel and space for about ten people and some equipment up front. There's just a two-man crew, taking us further and further out into the open sea off the far north-east coast of the Scottish mainland, where Caithness turns the corner to follow the north coast to Dounreay and Cape Wrath. Next to me Ewan is wedged onto the metal bench, holding on tight as saltwater arcs over us in a fine shower. It's his first time on open water and he's handling it pretty well, as are the other researchers in the boat, drawn by the opportunity to visit an oil graveyard otherwise invisible to the world. Up front Linda clings to the bow, having piggybacked on the charter when she learned we were back in Caithness. Next to her, Magnus from the nuclear plant is wrapped in oilskins and taking the worst of the spray to starboard. He's a brave man – ten hours before he had been at a birthday celebration in a Thurso pub, about to head to his bed, when he got a call from me giving him the green light.

William is making for a set of abandoned oil platforms 24km away as the crow flies. This is a two-hour sailing in a normal boat but the RIB can do it in about half that. The only problem is that the vessel needs to move along the plane of the waves, slowing it down as we zigzag back and forth to avoid the full force of the swell. The boat is fast but vulnerable and this is really at the limit of where it can operate.

'If you were members of the public I wouldn't bring you out here', William shouts as another wave batters into the port side. It's easy to see why – this is hardly a pleasure cruise, and the weather is dubious. Safe, but not comfortable, as William had diplomatically put it when he messaged me to say we had a window. Me and Ewan had been on standby in Glasgow for weeks, waiting to go, nervously watching the ocean weather forecast. When the call came we threw our wet-weather kit and research materials into the back of the car, watching the 270 miles of Highland tarmac tick down as we headed north again, desperate to make it out before the next front came in and the opportunity vanished. By the time the single CD in the glovebox had cycled round for its third play Ewan turned it off, preferring the roar of the wind across eastern Sutherland in the dusk on the last stretch to Wick and the boat.

From land the platforms are just visible as little square lumps on the surface of the North Sea, but with every wave they grow impossibly larger. When I think we are close

William tells us we are still fifteen minutes out. It is only as the boat draws near and he cuts the engine that the patchwork of gantries and doorways shows its true size, steel mountains pushing up from hidden depths without any reference points. The side of the rig is like an empty opera stage, levels upon levels of lights, corridors, ladders and winch cables exposed for the world to see. This is a place that once teemed with people, but as the boat bobs on the rolling surfaces there is only the splash of the water on the platform legs, the taste of salt in the air and a faint smell of rust and industrial paint.

The only reason we can get up this close is because the rig is decommissioned and normal shipping is allowed to approach it. Even then William has to go back and forth on the radio to give warning that we are in the area. Operating oil and gas rigs are subject to strict shipping restrictions and exclusion zones for reasons of safety and national security, and most of them are too far out to reach in anything other than a trawler or a supply boat. When the rigs were being assembled in the 1970s there was no standard blueprint, so while oil and gas wells on land are often little more than a derrick surrounded by a security fence, out in the North Sea each well required its own village. The two Beatrice platforms resemble an oil tanker sliced into sections and reassembled at random, welded onto stilts turning orange with rust around the joints and rivets.

Beatrice was named for the second wife of a maverick Texan oil baron who wanted to mark the occasion of their engagement, a change from the more prosaic names that dot the North Sea map. For the people who work offshore, labels like Claymore, Brent, Ninian and Miller carry memories of different faces, mess rooms, bunks and flight times. Speak to North Sea veterans and they will tell you the best and worst platforms, the most extreme storms they have experienced, and the reality of going on shift in the dark to keep the oil and gas flowing far from the kitchens and motorway service stations where it ends up.

Ewan and I had spent a lot of time writing about oilfields and interviewing riggers without ever visiting one. Our requests to oil companies to do fieldwork on offshore supply boats had been ignored, and getting on the helicopters out to the rigs is even harder. I'd spent a year phoning and emailing people up and down the east coast, from private yachts to off-season ferry skippers. In Shetland a boat had agreed to take me out to the Ninian field only to turn around and demand £15,000 a day when they realised it was for university research. Unsurprisingly, the finance department had said no. Eventually we had decided our best bet was Beatrice, and William, a veteran deep-water skipper who had spent most of his career guiding container ships from Scandinavia to Greenland.

He'd asked if we had any equipment. When people hear the word research they imagine wind readings and water samples, dropping lines to the sea bed and sealing marine life into collection jars. All we wanted to do was go and have a look. He'd never had a request like that before, but he also fancied the challenge of taking the boat right out to the rigs.

We do a few loops of the platforms and take photos, and William runs through the trivia he knows best; depths, seabird populations and weather conditions. As the wind drops for a minute you can hear the rigs creak, shifting slowly on their legs. What we can see above the waves is only half of the total height of the platforms. Under the seabed are layers of sediment and rock, and under that the pockets of the remaining petrocarbons that are not worth drilling for.

We'd wanted to stay longer, to loop out round to see the remains of a dismantled injection platform that pumped water into the reservoirs and pushed oil towards the well-heads, but as we float in the shadow of the platforms William casts an eye out to sea and a bank of cloud on the horizon. The wind is already picking up and he pushes the wheel hard to starboard and points the nose of the boat back to Wick, shouting for us to hold on. Ewan is starting to shiver, and a wave comes over the bow and hits the radio mic. It briefly fizzles and then dies, sign enough that we need to get home and get warm.

After fifty years of North Sea oil the east coast of Scotland should be one of the wealthiest regions in Europe, but Wick is a town still waiting for something to happen. On the main street shops lie empty, robbed of customers who no longer exist. The railway station is deserted save for the low rumble of the breeze through the rafters. Outside tourist season it costs the government far more to run trains than is brought in from ticket sales. Two of the most deprived neighbourhoods in the country are a short walk from the harbour, with income levels that would make headlines in the city and lead to task forces and talk of urban segregation.

People will tell you of the days when the fishing fleets were so big you could walk from one side of Wick harbour to the other by jumping from deck to deck, and trains of herring would go south carrying vans packed with fish. Unlike Thurso, where the nuclear plant and the port have given the town a surer footing, Wick is the future seen through a glass darkly. Now, in midwinter, it feels a long way from the petro-wonderland of luxury homes and wooden-lined boardrooms of oil wealth. The rain moves at forty-five degrees, dipping into the closes and wynds as I make my way through town and down to the quayside, dodging trucks and bulk loaders. I'm heading for a pristine building looking out over the harbour that stands out amongst the derelict shells on the hill behind.

The door intercom buzzes and Andy appears, the firm handshake of a former offshore worker masquerading as that of an office man out of place among the potted plants and fitted carpets of the reception desk. I sign the log-in book, leaving my signature just as I've done countless times before at offices and security booths across the country. Time in, time out, organisation, contact number, person visited.

This is the other side of Beatrice. When the oilfield was shutting down it was turned into a test site for offshore wind, one of the first projects in Europe. The trials showed that not only could wind turbines be put up, but they would stay up and produce impressive energy yields. It was the beginning of the offshore gold rush in Scotland and showed people around the world what was possible.

The inside of the wind-farm control centre is the pragmatic architecture of the new Scotland – energy-efficient windows, LED lights, comfortable chairs and electric heating, clean, bright and inviting but still straight out of a catalogue. Andy shows me into a side room and we sit down. I put my coat on the back of the chair and he moves it to the hatstand in the corner so that the water doesn't soak into the wood veneer on the arms.

'See the team upstairs? That's eleven guys, and eight of us have come from an oil and gas background. The vast majority is local guys who've been brought up here, moved away to work, and they've decided it's time to come back home and get a living', Andy says when I have the replacement microphone on and running. The one that drowned in the sea spray was only fit for the bin.

The Beatrice windfield is just to the north of the old rigs and has 84 turbines, each 288m high from the base of the jackets under the surface of the North Sea to the top of the blade. Andy has to send out teams to each of them whenever something goes wrong, but just keeping them going in the extreme conditions is a challenge. 'In summer we can have forty guys out there on the boats doing maintenance', he says, gesturing towards the harbour out of the window. 'You have a window, and you use that window.'

Beyond Beatrice two more wind fields are rising from the seabed, even taller and more powerful. Ewan and I had gone to see the fabrication yards in Nigg down the coast, taking photos in front of new turbine heads the size of a small house, ready to be lifted into place by a crane ship adapted from an oil tanker.

The control centre is a cosy affair, squeezed into the upstairs room of the dock-front house. It is a considerably more pleasant place to work than an oil rig, insulated and close to home. The room is a patchwork of screens and monitors, the ops team sitting in ergonomic chairs so they can swivel to read off the information. Screens show output, weather maps, shipping, turbine efficiency and grid load. A network of long-range CCTV cameras lets the onshore team check on each individual turbine without having to send a reluctant engineer out in the middle of a gale.

A few months later I will open the BBC website and see a picture of the Prime Minister, UK Energy Secretary and leader of the Scottish Labour Party in the same spot, carefully posing for a photographer who has jammed himself between the wall and the bank of computer screens to give the impression that the politicians are gazing intently at the live schematics. History doesn't always repeat itself but it does circle round a few times before moving on, and London is suddenly keen to see what the north of Scotland can do for the rest of the UK.

Andy runs through the figures, the cable lengths and wind speeds, maximum and average output. The ops centre has about thirty jobs attached to it, and as many again in the support from external companies who run the dedicated boats and emergency response. It's a fraction of the work on a rig, but in Wick it's welcome. The wind farm paid for an upgrade of the harbour, and for the first time in a while there is plenty of traffic. Andy asks me not to take any photos – the place is privately owned but the whole operation is a critical piece of national infrastructure.

Ten years before Beatrice began generating energy many were unsure whether deep-water turbines were even possible, and doubts were raised about how quickly they could be developed. Oil and gas companies spent the same period pushing for old oil wells to be used for carbon capture and storage (CCS), where the fossil gases are pumped back into the bedrock, sealed off from the atmosphere. In that time not a single CCS operation has been successful in Scotland, while Beatrice and the two adjacent wind fields rising from the seabed can turn out more energy than a nuclear power station.

In the early days of oil, conditions in the North Sea were such a barrier to energy extraction that overcoming them became a point of pride. Engineers pushed themselves to go deeper and further, with wells that had previously been considered impossible to sink or not financially viable coming online through new drilling techniques, GPS-guided drill-heads and sensors developed by NASA to work in space which were just as useful under the seabed. When North Sea oil was first discovered in the 1960s it began a space race to develop the technologies to pump it out and get it ashore.

In a few short years some of the biggest rigs ever constructed were bolted and welded together in the shallow firths of the Scottish coast and floated out to the newly discovered oil and gas wells. The window for getting them built and anchored above the pump sites was minimal, limited to the summer months when they could be safely towed out. Even then, in an age before computer modelling and stress testing, nobody knew whether they would stand up to the battering they faced, a hundred kilometres or more out and exposed to saltwater spray and rain that can move upwards. Some rigs never ever made it to drilling sites, sinking where they sat in bad weather or due to design faults.

It's an irony that as oil companies have tried to rebrand carbon, the skills they pioneered to find fossil fuels in the North Sea have proven perfect for building wind turbines as high as the rigs they replaced. Concrete piles, steel jackets, cranes that stabilise in rough water, deep-sea cable and conduit laying, helicopter winchmen and industrial electricians, survey boats and offshore supply vessels with experienced skippers. These are the hands and tools of a new economy on the bones of the old.

Wind isn't easy – in the control room one of the service techs tells me about the sinking feeling when a turbine fault means they have to physically go out. The service catamarans have a rubber prow and the skippers have to caress the throttle until the brow kisses the base of the turbine jacket at water level. The engineer then takes a running jump onto the ladder before the boat pulls away, climbing to the service platform where the turbine door is. Once inside there is a mechanical winch, and the tech will have to go up a hundred metres to reach the turbine head where the generators are located. If the fault is bad they can fly in mechanics or special-ist electricians, and if a serious failure occurs the whole thing comes offline, is demounted and replaced.

Accidents happen, but I'm reminded of what another renewables engineer had said to me in Orkney. If a wind turbine breaks in a storm then you have an expensive repair job that costs the company millions in lost revenue, but at least the sea doesn't catch fire. In my coat pocket I have a safety chit given to me by the first mate of an offshore supply vessel (OSV), the sort used on rigs and the OSV boats to register anything that might pose a risk. The official line in the oil industry is that safety is always a priority, but accidents are hugely expensive as well. Around the world oil companies are fighting long and hard to reduce their liabilities from spills and leaks, and the health impacts on oil workers who have spent their adult lives exposed to petrochemicals.

Nobody owns the seabed once you venture beyond the coastal envelope, but equally nobody could legally drill for oil without the permission of the states controlling the exclusive eco-nomic zones that run for two hundred nautical miles from land. The North Sea is split down the middle between the Scottish and Norwegian zones. Although you can see the Norwegian rigs from the British ones, because of how Norway structured its industry what happens with the profit is very different. This is what allowed the Norwegians to channel as much money as possible from oil back into the public purse. Britain, on the other hand, ended up letting multina-tional energy companies drive the industry for private profit. The two sides of the North Sea are like parallel universes. What was lost in the 1970s can never be returned, vanished into tax breaks and foreign bank accounts. Baudelaire said the greatest trick the devil ever pulled was making people forget he existed, and the UK oil industry is much the same.

Working offshore is not for the weak-willed. Pay can still be good but it means signing over to a military regime of rising, eating, working and sleeping on repeat for weeks. You're on the rig until your seat is booked off it on the helicopter back to the mainland, and if the weather turns or the helicopters fail then you're stuck far out in the open sea on a creaking and slowly moving metal hulk.

It's lunchtime when I walk through the doors of the terminal at Aberdeen airport. In the upstairs departure lounge rows of men in casual sportswear sit listening to wireless headphones, their faces fixed on tablets and laptop screens. Outside, the high-pitched whine of the helicopter engines is constant, and there's a faint smell of aviation fuel on the wind. The internet has made life offshore a touch more manageable, and the guys flying in and out can now take their world with them. One technician getting ready to fly out to Shetland told me that when you're in the helicopter lounge you start to go into what he called 'game mode', shifting into a work cycle that begins as soon as you step onto the helipad in the survival suit all helicopter passengers must wear.

As the flights are called and the riggers rise from their chairs to head towards the tarmac, a fresh stream of arrivals come out, some straight off a night shift. The helicopters fly multiple runs each day, out and back, stopping only to refuel and swap worn, tired bodies for fresh labour. Running choppers is expensive, and to keep profit margins up they're used intensively. The operators have scaled back their operations again and again, loaning a mantra from the low-cost airline industry that an aircraft on the ground is losing money and an aircraft in the air is making it. The whole of the Scottish side of the North Sea is serviced by fewer than thirty aircraft.

Rigs are also dry, and the nearest pub to the Aberdeen helicopter terminal is set up for customers who want to eat a square meal of their own choosing and sink a few jars. Spiders, as it is known colloquially, has a sign in the bar asking inbound workers to stack their kit bags in the designated area to leave room around the pool table and dartboard. On one wall a line of fruit machines does a steady trade, and the barman pours amber pints of lager before they have been ordered.

Stevie and Roger are both two drinks in when we get chatting, one in his early fifties looking forward to getting home to see his new granddaughter, the other just turned thirty and quieter, chipping in every now and then between trips to the front door for cigarettes. They're from Merseyside, expert scaffolders who spend their time harnessed up, building temporary structures above the waves for maintenance and inspections. A rig can have hundreds of workers on it, but only a small proportion are actually responsible for extracting the oil or gas. Once the well is sunk and the product is flowing the main purpose of riggers is to keep the platform safe and intact, monitoring, maintaining and repairing. There are scaffolders, stewards, helicopter ground staff, medics, chefs, drill-head technicians, pump technicians, safety officers and electricians. The rig is an ocean liner that never moves.

'Sometimes when you've been off and you go back into the weather it takes you a while to adjust', says Roger, as Stevie rolls another cigarette. 'And there's times when you ask yourself whether this is safe. Someone will tell you it is safe and that you need to go out and get on with the job, but you know yourself when it's too much.'

Stevie points up at the fruit machine. 'The guy who was just there was managing us, but we come in and out and if we report something he knows we're off the rig again and maybe not back ever again.'

There's a disdain in his voice, for the individual and the company. North Sea workers work for disparate contractors and subcontractors, with increasingly weak protections and lowered liabilities for the people who actually own the platform. If you ask too many questions or make too much trouble they can just bring in someone else. 'He just tells us it isn't a problem because he'll do anything he can do avoid shutting down production. I'd punch him in the face if I could', adds Stevie bitterly.

The North Sea has also had its fair share of disaster. In 1988, when the Piper Alpha platform exploded after a gas jet ignited, 165 workers and two rescuers lost their lives, but it was by no means the first North Sea accident. In 1980 a Norwegian rig had capsized in bad weather, killing 123. Blowouts send oil cascading into the water, and there have been hundreds of smaller leaks and accidents that often don't even merit news reporting. After Piper Alpha the oil companies changed their practice to make sure multiple members of the same family were not on the same rota.

Oil workers are more complex than the stereotypes. Life on the rig gives you a new grammar and access to a certain poetry. One guy I had interviewed who was out in the Ninian field paid his way through film school using oil wages. He described sneaking out of the leeward side of the rig in a storm when everyone was supposed to be on shift or tucked up in their bunks, feeling the platform shift under him in a figure of eight with the swell stretching its tentacles up the legs of the rig.

'There's no horizon, no scale, no reference points. It's just you and the heaving grey of the water.'

Oil companies like to portray the people on the rigs and the people in the boardrooms as one and the same, all working to supply customers with energy against the elements. In reality the rig workers and the money men live in different worlds entirely. A large chunk of the relatively generous pay packets is – in Stevie's words – danger money. Oil rigs are factory colonies and there are the broken legs, chemical burns, respiratory problems from repeated hydrocarbon exposure and mental health issues. During the pandemic, rigs with positive COVID-19 cases were put into rolling lockdowns and two-week stays turned into months. Riggers often report dissociation as they try to marry their life in the surreal offshore seascape with the return to the domestic that follows. Like veterans discharged from the military, they can also come home wondering what and for whom they have been fighting.

There's a reason the rigs are dry and personnel are regularly tested for drugs. Caffeine, nicotine and antidepressants are all allowed, but in The Spider pupils dilate as amber lager sparks to life the receptors deep in the brain after the dry weeks. In the bars in central Aberdeen you can find a wrap of cocaine or MDMA easily enough, and as much alcohol as you can handle and afford.

'The thing is, if I wasn't doing this I'd be a scaffolder in Liverpool on half the money', says Stevie, as he heads outside for another smoke. Oil is one of the last industries in Britain where medium-skilled manual labourers can earn decent middle-class wages. By the time they are in their mid-twenties offshore crew can own houses and buy cars, go on holiday twice a year and put cash away for retirement. Oil is hard to automate, both for reasons of safety and technical complexity, and that means good jobs for the people prepared to do them.

Everything is aimed towards one single focus, the extraction of the product from the seabed to land, to the refineries, and finally to the market. Oil workers are merely the first link in a chain, and as the profit margins shrink pieces of the industry are being hived off. Rigs are owned by investment funds who contract operations to another party. They in turn will pay other subcontractors. A huge chunk of the people who work on the rigs have no formal relationship with the owners or the big oil companies; they work for the tellingly named human-resource providers, everything costed to maximise profit and reduce outlays. The oil industry likes to talk about a sustainable transition – which also means sustainable profits – and pushes a vision of gas as a transition fuel, trying desperately to prevent its North Sea rigs becoming expensive stranded assets.

Oil has come to power our world because it is simple – you put it in barrels and each barrel has a value, and you trade the barrels like any other commodity. Renewable electricity is trickier, because it's potentially everywhere but you have to find something to do with it. Hydrocarbons have chemical energy locked into them, waiting to be released as heat and light, but when you use the wind or the sea to turn generators that produce electricity you can't just package it up and ship it to customers.

The global oil supply is heavily regulated to keep profits up. Too much fossil fuel and the market value plummets; too little and people begin to look for alternatives. With electricity you can produce power wherever you have kinetic or heat energy. Scotland already produces more electricity than it can use, and in theory still has thousands of gigawatts of untapped offshore potential.

Winter has turned again when I come back to Wick, heading north to do a few more interviews as the dark, hard months of intense teaching and damp cold come to the city. I realise this is my fifth time back in Caithness in the space of a year, sleeping in a small rented flat above a closed shop in Wick. The memory card on the radio microphone is already near-full. The storms are knocking at the door of the harbour again, trying to get in. Further down the coast there have been slices of cliff torn off and the stone barrier that separates the sea and the town has a large crack in it, which somebody needs to pay for.

If you have any doubts about the sheer power of the North Sea, then standing on the rocks at the harbour entrance in the small, dark months will quickly make them disappear. I have a friend who researches interactions between humans and marine life and swims off the east coast year round, immune to the cold and expert at reading the swell so that she bobs with the rising and falling water instead of working against it. Once I went in with her and lasted all of two minutes. Half an hour later she waded up the beach with a knowing smile as I shivered in a thick Shetland jumper, perched on the open car boot. She tried to make me feel better by telling me about the times she has got into trouble, south-westerlies riding in with rising waves that carried her six feet in the air and straight into the breakwater. She got out by clawing her way along the damp stonework until she felt the longshore drift under her feet and could pull herself onto the beach. She says it's a sober reminder that beyond the carefully choreographed social media pictures of wild swimming and windswept beaches under crisp winter skies, the sea will kill you if you give it the chance.

Most people will never visit this small corner of a small country, even as they burn gas in their homes and oil in their cars, or use wind energy in their widescreen TVs and air fryers. The lanes of the old town are empty as I walk around the harbour rim to the training platform where the wind engineers practise jumping onto the ladders of the turbine jackets. The swell is high and I look over to where William's boat is usually moored up at the pontoon. She's out of the water, tucked away for the worst half of the year on a trailer. Somewhere an engine splutters and the rev of the diesel train in the desolate railway station marks the arrival of a handful of people from Inverness, changing places with a few making the slow journey back south again in the black. Caithness steels itself for snow, and out across the waves the wind makes the turbines dance in a ring around Beatrice's rusting oil hulks.

9

The social forest

The spring snows are still dusting the tops when I drive up the road through Glencoe and round past the narrows at the top of Loch Linnhe. I've driven this way so many times I know exactly where to brake and accelerate, where to look out for tourists wandering aimlessly into the highway, and what time of day to set off for a clear run. Each trip I'm on my way somewhere new, heading for Skye or Mallaig to take the boat west, or for the mountains of the central West Highlands with the microphone on the passenger seat and my medication bag in the glove compartment.

Every year hundreds of thousands of tourists pack into hire cars and tour buses from Edinburgh and Glasgow to the West searching for a slice of wild Scotland, drawn by algorithmically selected visuals and the promise of spiritual emancipation on the open road. The Scottish government explicitly encourages mass tourism and boasts about the number of visitors who engage with the national brand. Influencers punt everything from hotel stays to home furnishings and entirely average restaurants in exchange for money on their social media accounts.

Even with the tourists crowding the roadside this is a beautiful place. The Glencoe viewpoint is a reliable spot to find pensioners from England, Chinese tourists taking choreographed romantic photos with elaborate lighting rigs, and Americans looking for a connection to an older landscape. It's one of the most photographed locations in the British Isles, a huge wall of rock on the main road down to the sea where the light flashes through the glen.

The huge open moor at Rannoch on the way up to Glencoe and Fort William blows people away the first time they drive across it. The night train up from London uses this section of line in its advertisements, beautiful people in early middle age waking up and lifting the blind to see deer by the fenceless tracks and snow-topped peaks from the warmth of their beds.

There's something that doesn't quite sit right, though. Scotland's wilderness is more a product of its geography than great remoteness. The distance from Glasgow to Fort William is less than New York to Philadelphia or London to Southampton. It should take ninety minutes by car or train, but nobody has ever found the money to blast roads and railways through the mountains like the Norwegians or the Austrians, where you can hop from one side of the Alps to the other quicker than you can drink a glass of wine from the buffet car. Scotland is a small country made to feel big; there are no straight lines and the roads need what is euphemistically called an active driving style. People I know who grew up in the West have the gear-changing skills of pro rally drivers and a flexible approach to speed limits. On the two-lane highway you can spot the local contractors in Ford vans and people on their way to work in battered pickups, dipping in and out of the campervans and tourist buses flocking to see the magic of the Scottish lochs and glens.

I feel terrible – the doctor has put me on new medication and I haven't slept more than three hours a night for a week, though the insomnia does make it easier to drive. Even if I want to fall asleep I can't. I feel like Harvey Keitel in *Death Watch*, who takes 'unsleeping pills' paid for by his employers to stay awake and filming. I'm told it will settle down once my brain adjusts; in some ways it's a welcome change from the drowsiness of nerve suppressants and painkillers. I decided I'd rather be on the road doing fieldwork than lying awake in a flat in a Glasgow staring at the ceiling.

The research was never supposed to be therapeutic, but listening to the lives of others is a very good way to see your own more clearly. There's a multitude of people and places out in the world, and it's helpful to remember you're just one person drifting through it.

The road up the coast begins at the bottom of my street in Glasgow and carries on all the way to the top of Skye. It's a tapestry of old drovers' paths and military routes that were joined together to form what the government claims is a major trunk route. On the map it looks like a well-planned artery; only when you actually sit behind a wheel and travel the thing do you see it for what it is, but for all its difficulty it is also one of the most beautiful drives in Europe, touching the Firth of Lorne and Linnhe before looping back up and through the Kintail hills, finally hitting the sea again at Loch Duich and Loch Alsh. I'm not going as far as Skye this time, peeling off inland before the road drops back to the sea. My destination a little dot on the map in Glenmoriston, north-west of Loch Ness.

I first came here a decade ago on a story, given the task of producing something for a German TV channel on the attempts to bring back beavers and wolves to the landscape. Glenmoriston is in many ways unremarkable, and most people will pass straight through it without stopping. On a hot day the River Moriston is good for a swim and when the local dams let their water out on Tuesdays the levels rise and you can run the rapids, seeing the flow as it would have been before the hydro boys got their hands on it.

Halfway up the glen and just before the dam there's a turn-off that leads into a gravel car park. I pull off the road and up the slope into a spot under the trees. The gravel is freshly laid and on one side of the neatly marked spaces EV chargers sit waiting for the electric cars that are yet to mainstream. I look back at the ancient Honda. The brand new electric equivalent costs twelve times as much, and isn't getting any cheaper. The advertisements show silent cars gliding through empty cities and along well-maintained mountain roads, as if soon the whole world will be Switzerland. Ahead is a low lodge, couples in expensive outdoor gear milling around outside drinking coffee, or strolling under the trees.

After four hours in the car it feels as if I've walked into someone else's dream. Dundreggan is a place that has seen life come and go several times. A sporting estate that lost its house to fire, it ended up in the hands of a wealthy Italian business magnate who died with nobody else willing to take it on. In his twilight years he was said to favour sitting on the veranda of the pebbledash 1960s hunting lodge with his carbine, waiting for deer to wander into view before dispatching them from the comfort of his chair.

Scotland's aristocracy no longer run an empire, but a private Scottish estate is a sought-after accessory for the modern billionaire. Middle Eastern and Russian fossil money has meant large tracts of land being hived off to people who want to entertain their friends and business partners like Victorian lairds, but they also want a castle to go with their hunting and fishing rights. Dundreggan has no Disney castle, but it has something far more valuable. At the back of the car park and through a deer fence is one of the few remaining patches of ancient forest in Scotland, a remnant of a time seven thousand years ago when the hills and glens of the Highlands were covered in trees that sustained a complex web of plant and animal life.

The Caledonian Forest pre-dates the human settlement of Scotland – its trees migrated north after the Ice Age and adapted to the local temperature range, forming a dense band from the Atlantic to the North Sea that thrived in the damp glens and co-created a whole new ecosystem. This Scottish variant of the taiga that straddles the sub-arctic and arctic from Alaska to Scandinavia was home to bears, lynx, wolves, beavers and elk. Then people arrived, and with them came a terraforming of the landscape that accelerated as demand for timber and farmland grew. This was worsened as modernity came to Scotland by the politics of landownership, with the Highlands being cleared of smallholders and agriculture for large-scale sheep farming and hunting estates, and an explosion in deer with no natural predators.

The Dundreggan remnant is still incredibly fragile – young trees are in a constant battle to grow strong enough to resist invasive deer and the weather. The tiny patch of dense forest at the site is carefully safeguarded, fenced in for its own safety by a charity who have set up Scotland's first dedicated rewilding centre. The reserve also has a nursery that produces seedlings that can be boxed up and taken to other restoration sites.

Inside the centre feels like an alpine ski lodge; teenagers make cappuccinos behind the counter and groups of walkers scan maps for the hikes they have planned during their lunchtimes behind London office desks. For a lot of people the idea of being in wilderness is as important as actually experiencing it, and the centre has a series of easy trails that loop up through the forest with views back across the glen. The chef has made some wild nettle pesto and is spooning it onto plates with venison pies and home-made salads.

'Do you work here? I think I've seen you before', says the café manager, a woman in her late forties supervising the teenagers at the coffee machine. I explain what I'm doing, pointing to the microphone in my hand and the battered car through the window. It's less formal and glamorous perhaps than what people expect, but so much of research is just about drifting and watching. We find out we have a common friend, a guy named Doug who retired from Dundreggan after a career spent trying to save birds and threatened habitats. I've known his daughter since we were sixteen when we met in the sticky darkness of a music venue near King's Cross station in London. She became an environmental artist and I became an environmental journalist, and she was the one who first told me about Dundreggan. In Scotland you're never more than three people removed from anyone else.

In one of the classrooms attached to the café the chairs are askew from a training session. Things are accelerating as the charity has scaled up. The climate crisis means reforestation has never been more pressing, or more popular.

Gwen, the Dundreggan Estate manager, directs me in to one of the small classrooms, apologising for the small window between meetings. The communications officer for the charity had suggested we chat online, until I explained I wanted a chance to come back to Dundreggan again and see what had happened since I was last in the woods of Glen Moriston. After the pandemic researchers started to do more and more interviews by video call, imagining that the flat faces of a laptop screen could act as substitute for the full contours of real life. When you visit people where they stand you see what they do and say in full colour, and get answers to questions you would never have thought to pose.

I can't place Gwen's accent, so I ask her.

'Belgian', she says, the Flemish blending into the softer vowels of Scottish English. It makes sense as soon as she tells me. My accent's similarly vague – an adult life spent in Scotland and Sweden, with the tell-tale traces of my mum's Derbyshire vowels and well-pronounced Sussex consonants of primary school. We're all hybrids at the end of the day, made up of multiple life and multiple lives.

Climate change and the simmering unease it brings means rewilding has exploded in the last few years. The mega-projects of Sutherland and the Flow Country are one part of the movement, but Dundreggan was the first place I had ever seen it come together in practice, a growing movement of conservation experts and volunteers with a clear vision for nature restoration and increasing political support. The estate describes itself as a flagship, an example of what can be done with time, energy and money.

'What we are now calling rewilding has been going on for a long time', Gwen points out when I ask about the new Rewilding Centre and the influx of visitors sipping coffee across the hallway. Dundreggan is a popular visitor destina-tion, and Gwen's job is to manage the whole estate, far up the hill from the education displays and guided walks. She came to Dundreggan from a career in habitat conservation, and though the centre is brand new, the seeds of projects like Dundreggan were sown long before it became mainstream. Climate and conservation campaigners put in the hard yards through the 1990s and 2000s to try and move the debate on from bringing back single species and declaring national parks to wholesale landscape restoration, showing the interdependencies that climate science has proven to be more and more important. Trees for Life, the charity that runs Dundreggan, is over thirty years old, founded two years before the first ever UN climate COP. The world is just catching up.

Dundreggan is enchanting – I've had the good luck to always be here in good weather when the sun soaks the clearings in golden light and scatters through the canopy onto the ferns below – but it takes a while to understand what it is you have in front of you beyond the obvious. Forests are complex places; when I last visited Doug had sat down with me under the canopy of the trees and explained what was happening out of sight below ground, in the water table and the soil and the mycorrhizal networks and root systems that bind the habitat together.

The forest has its own sociology well away from humans, multiple species and forms of life relying on other another and interacting. The biggest known single organism on earth – a colony of *Armillaria ostoyae*, or honey fungus – runs through the forest floor in the Pacific US for miles, killing trees but also creating conditions for new growth as they decay and thin. Scotland has very few places where tree cover is extensive enough for such a large network, but like the viruses reproducing invisibly in our bodies, forests are assemblages in which the trunks and canopy are merely the most visible part.

Trees absorb atmospheric carbon, but it is fungi and bacteria that help to lock it into the soil through exchange with living plants. When trees die they can rot and release carbon into the atmosphere again, but in well-maintained and diverse forest systems that carbon can also be locked into the soil more permanently. Older, long-lived forests store carbon more effectively, and governments have begun to realise that healthy forests are valuable like never before. The enthusiasm for what climate planners call nature-based solutions increases as more and more schemes begin to show success, building on the ability of natural systems to recover once the stepping stones are in place. Schemes to reintroduce native species like beavers and lynx are based on the keystone and biodiversity-boosting role that they play, but like the funguses slowly targeting the weak trees and providing soil nutrients, they both kill and produce life. Beavers fell trees and create natural dams and firebreaks, while lynx scare away deer. Rewilding is about repeopling too; one of the biggest successes of the Dundreggan site, alongside its reforestation and rewilding work, has been the creation of sustainable local jobs at the Rewilding Centre. It's a very different story to the green lairds and private rewilding projects found elsewhere.

Gwen tells me how Dundreggan holds remnants of sheilings – the traditional cottages once used for summer grazing by families from crofting townships. These seasonal dwellings were in use until the mid-18th century, when the land was cleared for sheep farming during the Highland Clearances. By the mid-19th century, land use had shifted again, this time to sport hunting for deer. Depopulation and limited employment opportunities remain challenges across the Scottish Highlands, and wherever you go in the glens around Loch Ness the shadows of the Highland Clearances are there in the undergrowth. Rewilding offers hope – creating local jobs, supporting sustainable livelihoods, boosting ecotourism and enabling communities to flourish.

'People need to be able to feel connected to the land', says Gwen, pointing out that rewilding is about restoring to the landscape the human relationships that have been lost. The reforestation movement in Scotland has always been closely linked to lingering questions about ownership and access.

Dundreggan is a living landscape, providing space for wildlife to flourish and communities to return in their wake.

The pace of change at Dundreggan is impressive, and the charity's ambition of large landscape-scale nature restoration is exciting. Eagles have begun nesting here again and biodiversity has blossomed. At the fringes of the forest remnant the trees are expanding slowly outwards. Above all else, perhaps, it is a place of possibility.

Resting under the trees of Dundreggan with the canopy full of birds and the saplings in the nursery, it's easy to get ahead of yourself. The project has been going for over a decade but climate change has created an urgency to the reforestation movement it cannot keep up with. Tree cover needs to increase massively worldwide to act as a carbon sink to even begin to check our emissions, and the planet is still experiencing net forest loss, largely due to commercial logging and the removal of rainforest for farming and development. The UN estimates that the net forest loss worldwide is around 4,000 sq km a year, an area bigger than Luxembourg. With it goes the most efficient form of carbon capture we have, irrespective of the poetic and aesthetic needs of the population for rugged beauty. Even if we can reach net zero in time to avoid further temperature rises, huge reforestation projects will be needed to put carbon back in the ground and take us back to pre-industrial levels and a stable global climate.

It's evening as I pack up my sleeping bag and tent and start the slow march up the hill, chasing the early April twilight. The sun begins to dip behind the ridge of Sail Chaorainn and the Kintail summits in the west. Each minute that I climb the hill the undergrowth begins to thin, past the foundations of the abandoned shielings and the last few young birches that have struck out on their own from the reserve. Soon I'm back on the bare moor with the green woods retreating behind me.

This is a big walk and I've tried to balance weight against the minimum of what might be needed. The more you carry, the harder it gets, and I no longer bring half the stuff I used to. I've come to realise that all you need is to rest softly and in the dry, to not go hungry and to have a way to make a warm drink. A colleague in California once told me how the science fiction author Kim Stanley Robinson would wander into the mountains of the Sierra Nevada with progressively smaller packs, experimenting to imagine the basics of survival on other worlds. One of the ironies of Scotland is that even where the ground is seemingly always wet and the trickle of water is ever-present, you may as well be on Mars. The landscape is often too degraded to naturally filter rainwater or is simply contaminated by livestock, and you have to either carry fresh water or filter or boil it to be sure you are not getting anything nasty.

As I go higher I am kept company by the deer eyeing me warily across the bare expanse and a set of 400,000v power lines built to take renewable energy from the Highlands to the south. It's part of the same system that runs all the way from Caithness to Glasgow; the engineers building it ploughed a swathe straight over the ridges and glens of the central Highlands against the wishes of the conservation lobby, and now Glenmoriston is the home of another technological megasystem to go alongside the Highland dams built eight decades before. The up side is that there are good hill tracks all the way. I cover the first few miles of ascent in less than an hour.

As the last sun goes I pitch the tent above Loch na Beinne Baine, a featureless oval of water stuck between two low summits, and climb inside. There are no animal sounds up here and the pylons are not the only thing that make the landscape feel industrial. The gravel tracks and the wind blowing freely across the hillside are reminiscent of a military test range. In the ground below, concrete-lined tunnels carry water to the turbines of the dam on the river. An ex-girlfriend of mine from the wooded hills of northern Greece used to always joke that you could take a picture of Highland Scotland and a picture of the surface of the moon in greyscale and you wouldn't be able to tell the difference. In California they paved paradise and put up a parking lot, but in Scotland they just demolished it without filling the gap.

Many people have never seen a true virgin landscape, and so we look at desolation and mistake it for wilderness. As I fall in and out of chemically interrupted sleep I try and imagine what it will be like when one day this is reforested too, terraformed into a place full of noise and life with the power lines dipping above the tree tops and sheltered places to sleep on the shore.

When I wake up at dawn there are inversions – warm air sits above cool air and the hills are clear, but the glens are thick with cloud and mist. Loch na Beinne Baine is only 500m above sea level, but it feels like 3,000 in the morning cold, compounded by the naked contours of the hills still in shadow, like waking up in the high Alps. I swing my legs out of the tent and fumble for my kettle flask, a portable electric cylinder that can boil fresh coffee without having to mess around with lighters and a gas stove in a storm. Pouring in condensed milk and instant coffee to make a bastardised Brazilian pick-me-up to go with my morning cocktail of medication, I'm surprised by just how alone I am. It is only twenty miles to the tourist traps of Loch Ness from here, but as I start the descent down towards Glen Affric nobody comes the other way out of the mist.

Glen Affric is Dundreggan's opposite number on the other side of the ridges, a whole valley where the Caledonian Forest has survived better than anywhere else in Scotland. The arbitrary nature of the deforestation is most apparent here, with wood and wire separating dense mature woodland on one side from open moorland with roaming deer on the other.

I know what I'm here to look at, but even so, the interior of my brain is flooded with an unexpected elation at the verdancy of the woods around. Helped by the coffee and the sugar, I feel a dopamine hit at walking through a gate and from the lunar wastes of the degraded moor into Arcadia. I am unapologetically and deliriously happy, as if the lights have just come back on after a power cut and suddenly a room of shadows is visible in full colour. This isn't the moist scent of the Scottish Highlands but the subtle mix of flavours and sounds of a Norwegian forest, familiar but in the wrong place.

As I move further into the glen I get to thinking about the American anthropologist Marshall Sahlins, who proposed that pre-modern societies were places of relative abundance, where people were able to satisfy a wide range of human need and where natural habitats were verdant in ways that are unthinkable to us today. Sahlins's theories are controversial, developed through observation of indigenous peoples with one eye firmly on modern politics, but his challenging of the belief that only industrial society is capable of providing high standards of material living is a fantastic provocation. Sahlins tried to show that hunter gatherers, in his words, 'pulled the lowest grades in thermodynamics', benefiting from the bounty of the natural landscape in a low-energy society in which work and leisure were not a binary.

Pre-agricultural societies had different understandings of land and property than even basic farming societies, Sahlins argued. You might own personal possessions or group tools, but the earliest humans to wander into the British Isles didn't see the forests around them as assets, merely context. Somewhere in the back of the brain is a little surviving remnant that recognises that.

It comes back to the very essence of what land is. Occupation is different from jurisdiction, and jurisdiction is different from ownership. The modern conception of property, where owners have title deeds and the ability to buy and sell their assets, is a relatively recent invention. A maverick land-justice campaigner I know who sat in the Scottish Parliament for a while once said something that has stayed with me: in the debates over who owns and manages Scotland's supposed nature, you rarely hear the unspoken truth that it needs to be owned by nobody but itself.

The slice of Scotland taking in Glen Affric and Dundreggan has been christened the Affric Highlands, with the ultimate aim of establishing a corridor of native forest running from the North Sea to the Atlantic with the glen at its centre. Dundreggan is working with private landowners, the government and other nature charities to turn a patchwork of different properties into one linked ecosystem. The whole scheme will be used as a laboratory for forest regeneration elsewhere, and once forests get going they become self-sustaining. Recovery is a passive and asymmetrical process as much as a rush for the finish line. The best thing we can do sometimes is just to take a step back.

One day this walk will take you a few days without ever leaving the woods, watched over by satellites calculating CO_2 absorption and monitored by teams of ecologists and hydrologists tracking the slow outward spread of the new Caledonian Forest from coast to coast. It may be built from the seedlings of a millennia-old remnant, but this is a new type of habitat entirely terraformed and cultivated as a place of safety in a time of global danger.

A good twenty miles out from Dundreggan my boots begin to eat into my toes, along with the very specific form of hunger that kicks in with a long hike. It doesn't sit in your stomach but in your legs and on your lips. The body needs water and energy before anything else. I'm glad I've got the quick boiler and a pack of Scotland's national chocolate bar, the caramel wafer. Hot caffeinated liquid and a few biscuits in your bag are a moveable feast. There's still some way to go as the pains start to move from my feet and up into my torso. I remind myself that there was a time I couldn't walk further than the end of the street without feeling like I would pass out. The pain is a welcome sign of good health.

A thirty-mile day is possible but not desirable, and even a twenty-mile day is a killer over bad ground. Even so, I want to get to my destination before the dusk sets in and before any snow has a chance to turn the wind to ice. I'm making for the far end of Affric, where the glen and its offshoots rise steeply to meet the Kintail hills in a series of ridges and the dense leaf cover falls away. The forest is starting to advance west, but as I begin the climb it becomes thinner and thinner until there are just a few bushes dotted across the boggy ground. I'm looking not for a forest but for a single tree, a survivor waiting for others to join it.

The Last Ent of Affric is an elm tree only reachable on foot from the glen, or via a tricky decent from the summit ridges, high up at the far end of the watershed with only itself and the open hillsides for company. The Ent gained its modern name from Tolkien's mythical ancient sentient race of trees, thanks to a facelike distortion in its trunk and the almost pathological desire to integrate the Scottish Highlands into the Anglo-Saxon cultural imaginary, but the tree is far older. How it ended up here is uncertain; like many remnants, it has kept on going in isolation over a few hundred years as invasive fungus has decimated the larger colonies elsewhere. Elms are hardy in other ways, and the annual snows and high winds have not bothered the Ent.

Elm doesn't burn well and warps, unlike oak, which is sought after for its strength and will keep a fire going for hours. For commercial forestry it has little worth, but elms are an important part of the diversity of old-growth forests. They create shelter, allowing smaller species to grow up around them. Animals visit, dropping more seeds, and wild flowers spring up as they drain the ground. The Ent is now surrounded by newly planted seedlings cultivated in the botanic garden in Edinburgh by forestry researchers, bred to be disease resistant and the first wave in a new self-propagating colony that will spread its offshoots back down towards the Affric remnant.

The sky starts to turn and I wonder how much further I have to go, when across the dark slopes I catch sight of the Ent, gazing up at the frozen horseshoes of the Kintail hills and the ridges leading to Mullach Fraoch-choire, 1,000m above sea level. In winter elms look half-dead, their pallid bark forming a black skeleton against the snow, but now in spring, with the snow limited to the higher ground, the Ent is beginning to come into leaf and the deeper green of the Highland summer bleeds in.

There's nobody else here, it's just me and the elm as I fall onto the grass, exhausted. I know I will sleep mercifully well before I even lay down my head on the groundsheet. I watch the dusk arrive and feel the air begin to chill before I crawl into my sleeping bag, and for the first time in weeks I dream. We lie there together, waiting for the forest to come back.

10

Plastic gods

Even at the start of summer the east coast of Scotland is usually cool, cut off from the Gulf Stream and fed by the Highland rivers that flow east and into the firths.

This year is different. A marine heatwave has created a pocket of warm air that pulls water from the sea before being pushed inland to the colder hills above central Scotland. On the wind come waves of rainstorms soaking the coastal towns of the east. We're in a gap between, bathed in a few hours of direct sunlight.

The promenade in Kirkcaldy has its share of dog walkers and skateboarders pretending that the breeze doesn't bother them, comforted by the fact it is at least sunny. They trek back and forth from the high-rise flats at the top of town to the site of the demolished coal mine at the bottom. The towers of the pitheads are long gone, replaced by a housing estate. The tunnels under the water are blocked and flooded, and there is not a working shaft between here and Russia now.

Keira pulls on her coat, climbing out of the passenger side of the Honda, her ginger hair blowing in her eyes and her scarf threatening to escape over the storm wall towards the beach. Offshore, tankers heading for the oil terminal at

Grangemouth are moored up in the deeper water of the Firth of Forth, waiting their turn.

We walk across empty car parks past boarded-up shops to a high stone wall visibly older than everything around it. From the other side the smell of unkempt grass and wet masonry drifts over. Like two teenage goths hanging around a churchyard we're looking for ghosts, or vampires, perhaps. Keira lives a few miles down the water in one of the increasingly bohemian coastal towns that have soaked up people fleeing the high prices and over-tourism of Edinburgh. She'd invited me for tea to see the new flat and I'd said yes on one condition – would she help me hunt for the ghost of Adam Smith?

Economics is a world of secular gods, and Adam Smith is the original prophet of modern globalised capitalism. The square of grass beyond the wall is a holy place for the disciples of free-market ideology. Here the devout come to seek the place where their Messiah walked.

Smith was born in Kirkcaldy in 1723, at the time a small coastal town with a fishing fleet and a few small industries, but coal capitalism was yet to hit Scotland with full force. As a teenager he went to study at the University of Glasgow, before moving on to Oxford, Edinburgh and the Continent. He never married and came back to Scotland to live with his mother again, in a house adjoining the garden where we're standing on tiptoes trying to see in. Looking out over the orchard towards the sea, Smith wrote *The Wealth of Nations*, the book that would become the sacred text of laissez-faire capitalism.

Adam Smith and Karl Marx bookended the Industrial Revolution, with less than a generation between them but living in different worlds. Smith saw the early stages of modern capitalism as a great liberator, once unleashed from the protectionism and cartelisation of the merchant system. Marx, on the other hand, saw capital as a beast to be tamed, capable of doing irreparable damage but, if taken from the hands of the rentiers and speculators, also as a means of social emancipation. Smith and Marx are less opposites than spectators viewing the same object from different times and directions, and what they share are dubious legacies and fanbases neither could ever have envisaged. In the 1970s and 1980s Smith became a symbolic counterweight to the perceived threat of communism and Soviet-led revolutionary Marxism, and patron saint of Thatcherism in the UK and Reaganism in the US. Today the cult of Smith continues as intellectual cover for the naked ideology of market fundamentalists and libertarians, but in the county of his birth the reception is more ambivalent. There is genuine pride at producing a founding father of the world economy, tempered by the bitter experience of Scotland being used as a laboratory for kamikaze free-market reforms by his self-appointed acolytes.

'My dad had a signed photo of Margaret Thatcher on his desk', Keira says as we peer over the wall, seeing little. 'He used to tell me it was my job to emulate her and become Britain's second female Prime Minister.'

Scotland is permanently torn between its two self-imagined ideals: the society of solidarity and shared suffering of the common man in an inhospitable country on the Atlantic fringe, and the success of individual graft and Protestant hard work. Ten miles west from Kirkcaldy you can visit the Andrew Carnegie birthplace museum and see where Carnegie lived in a one-room Scottish worker's cottage before he became one of the richest men in the world. He made untold wealth from railroads, oil and steel as part of the American industrial boom, the archetypal entrepreneurial Scot shaking hands merrily with all America had to offer.

Keira's family were in oil too, albeit as workers rather than owners. Her dad was on and off rigs, making money – as he saw it – from his own hard work and a head for an opportunity. He would lecture the family on the benefits of a stable income, of getting ahead and getting out. Oil was a new way of life that promised just that; Scots could now be like Texans – a big house, two cars in the driveway and a fitted kitchen. Oil was not just lucrative, it was also cosmopolitan, sophisticated, even.

Thatcher used North Sea oil to bankroll the economic reforms of the 1980s and the rise in unemployment that followed. North Sea oil was free-market economics' magic money tree. Oil was also integral to the new world Thatcherism and Reaganism envisioned, motorways and suburban estates based on homeownership and car ownership, matching leisurewear, Tupperware, plastic credit cards, polycarbide plastic CDs, home computers and mobile phones for yuppies, plastic bullets for Northern Ireland and an economy that embodied the dream of dynamic plasticity, fluid and flexible, moving at the speed of oil. Thatcher became a plastics research chemist after she graduated from Oxford, strongly believing that the future was made in the research laboratories of large private companies rather than the misguided paternalism of government.

Oil helped to build the new Britain of the 1980s and 1990s. Without oil there would be no car suburbs, no shopping centres filled with branches of the Disney Store and Pizza Huts, no luxury starter homes in the cul-de-sacs off cul-de-sacs off slip roads that flow from roundabouts, and no flights to Florida theme parks. I can remember sitting in a car on the way to an out-of-town cinema in the early 1990s for a friend's birthday party, asking his dad who he would vote for in the election I had heard adults talking about. He was an estate agent who had grown modestly wealthy off the Thatcher era's thirst for homeownership and skyrocketing house prices, drove a high-powered sports coupé and flew his family to Orlando for holidays. Without skipping a beat he turned to me from the front seat of the car and replied, 'Conservatives, buddy.'

'Mum and Dad had to burn their credit cards at one point and start again', says Keira as we walk up to the town museum to see Adam Smith's snuffbox, past the Adam Smith Theatre and a busker playing to an empty street. Keira's parents got caught by the bubble that made people feel rich and then made them feel poor just as quickly when debt collectors came knocking. 'But it was the eighties and I guess it was the dream of becoming middle class', she says. 'We grew up with no TV and ten pound a week to pay for food.'

In the centre of the Fife coalfield, Kirkcaldy was hit particularly hard by the intentional deindustrialisation and the end of manufacturing of the 1980s, something from which it has never fully recovered. The colliery at the south end of Kirkcaldy seafront closed in 1988. The site of Adam Smith's house has fared no better, now a derelict retail unit that last belonged to a discount bakery chain. The Enlightenment Hub – a visitor centre on the main street supposedly showcasing Smith's legacy – is shut, sublet as a returns office for an online retailer.

Though there were factories in Smith's Scotland there was nothing like the production lines, blast furnaces and hissing machinery that would define the country in the 1800s and that Marx experienced when he moved to Britain. Smith was interested in labour and efficiency, but what Marx saw that Smith did not was the steam engine and the automated mill as extensions of man in action. It was faster, stronger and cheaper production that could liberate normal people from the toil of work but also diminished them, making them bit-part players in someone else's profit margins. People became displaced from their labour, alienated from what they produced.

When oil and gas arrived in Scotland, Fife was made to benefit even though it was a long way from the oil heartlands. The pipelines from the north-east to the centre of the country flow through the fields behind the Fife coast and just as the Fife coalfield rumbled towards abandonment, new harbours and gas terminals were opened up, run by private energy giants rather than the government utilities. They had no need for miners but they did need chemical engineers and company men, locals for the menial jobs and trained incomers for the technical ones. The centre of the web was Mossmorran, a huge chemical plant just west of Kirkcaldy that I'd been trying to access without success.

Keira slides back into the passenger seat of the car and starts riffling through the CDs, complaining about the lack of a USB jack on my stereo to attach a smartphone. She examines and then dismisses each of the cracked cases in turn. After we drew a blank on the road to Wick I'd dug out what remained of my physical music collection from a storage unit under the Glasgow motorway bridges. She picks out an illegally burned CD covered with my chaotic teenage handwriting. 'What's this?' she asks.

I have no idea – the memory that held it is long gone and doesn't want to come back. My brain seems to have filtered out less useful parts of the past. I can barely read the writing, but it dates from the time when people I knew on music forums would send each other mix-CDs in the mail with handwritten sleeves and random finds from the depths of record-store shelves. We put the CD in and hope for the best. The laser hits the clear polycarbonate plastic and the petrol engine charges the battery that spins the disc. The speakers start to blare and we power on up the hill, off to find Mossmorran and the traces of Fife's fossil economy. The first track is turn-of-the-millennium American slacker rock played by men in zip hoodies and square glasses chastising George Bush and the World Bank.

As we leave town we pass a sign telling us the road is flooded. I slow down and look at Keira and she shrugs, so we carry on, assuming the council have just forgotten to remove the warning cones. There are cars coming the other way and a motorcyclist who looks dry. The storm the night before was heavy, but the sun is out and away from the coastal wind Fife feels like the Garden of England in July.

When we reach it the flood is a band of water ten metres long, stubbornly refusing to drain away at the bottom of a dip in the open farmland west of Kirkcaldy. 'It's your car', says Keira, absolving herself of any responsibility for what might happen. It is, all £2,000 of it. Whatever finally kills her is to be decided, but she's already inching towards the grave.

I rev the engine and let the injector do its work – the little explosions under the bonnet turn the pistons faster and faster as we enter the water. I try to hit it at a high enough velocity that even if the engine floods or we float free of the ground it should carry us over. The roads are in such a bad state that cars this small barely make it over the potholes, let alone the little lake in front of us. I pray there are no hidden craters under the surface.

The water drums against the doors and the bumper makes a wake before rising triumphantly out on the other side and onto dry land again.

We're through.

Then suddenly there's a clunk, and a grinding sound, and then the faint smell of petrol fumes. I'm filled with slow dawning regret at my own hubris. We roll to a stop in a farm gateway a hundred metres down the road and I jump out, sticking my head under the car to see whether we need to call a mechanic or a scrap merchant.

The exhaust has sheared off clean, pulled away by the force of the water and held on only by its rubber fastener. The pipe from the engine to the muffler is somewhere under the flood. I slide between the wheels and have to wrestle the remains of the muffler away with my hands, giving it a final tug like a farmer pulling potatoes triumphantly from the ground. I stand up again, cradling it in my arms, and Keira takes a picture. It finds a new home in the boot, a chimera of oil and rust worn to nothing by two decades of sea rain and the acidic mix of engine fumes that slowly corrodes the underside of the chassis.

The garage can't send anyone before the evening. Keira suggests I ring and tell them I have a pregnant woman in the car, or that my wife is ill and we can't be left out in the countryside. When we get through we're told to use the app of the insurance company that comes free with my credit card. Salvation is always ninety minutes away, until it starts to get dark and we realise that nobody is coming to save us.

We give up, creeping back down B roads and C roads with the engine misfiring and unfiltered petrol fumes leaking into the car. Keira is late for a party, and I am done. I dump the car on the forecourt of a local mechanic and write a note on the bonnet explaining I'll be back. My writing hasn't improved much since I wrote the track listings for the burned CDs, I note as I leave my mobile number, before walking wearily to the railway station and buying a ticket to Glasgow. The Mossmorran plant is there all the time across the cornfields, burning away on the horizon behind its high wire fences, glowing red in the summer night.

* * *

Eventually I do make it to the plant, the car patched up by a garage who offer discounts for cash purchases and take pride in keeping older models working with parts tracked down on the internet and pulled from salvage yards. This corner of Fife still has the tell-tale signs of an earlier era, narrow lanes and meadows, small copses on the hilltops and grazing cattle in sheltered inland valleys. The land around the Mossmorran chemical plant is no exception – I take a photo and send it to Ewan, the tall stacks of the facility standing proud in impossibly green fields under a perfectly blue sky. They remind me of Indiana grain silos jutting out of the plains on the drive up to Chicago from Cincinnati. It's good petro-pastoralism, the kind of photo you see in corporate social responsibility PR where the industry and nature harmoniously coexist.

The big sky makes the plant seem small, but as you move along the perimeter fence the pipework obscures the blue and the gas-venting stack grows impossibly large. The site is surrounded by cameras and wire fences – I take for granted that I'm now on the security databases of several large energy companies – and sure enough, a van begins to drive along the perimeter road to see what I am up to. The cameras have seen me get out and take pictures. Energy and petrochemical installations are more tightly guarded than anywhere I have ever been except for military bases, and even they were less secretive. You can walk up to a wind turbine or amble up to a dam unnoticed, yet the petrochemicals industry is its own kingdom, closed to the world by design and distilled so that all we see is the drip of petroleum from the fuel cap as we fill up our cars or rip plastic from plastic as we open trays of meat and toiletries. For something so central to the world we have made, we barely know it at all.

I can count the positive replies from oil companies to media and research requests over my career on one hand. Their preferred mode of engagement is carefully orchestrated visits and information sessions in hotel suites over buffet lunches. Once, together with a group of European energy journalists, I was given a tour of the Nordstream terminal on Germany's Baltic coast, pumping Russian gas into the heart of Europe, after being taken through its benefits by a well-practised PR man over lunch. I still have the expensively produced photobook I was given, *Sichere Energie für Europa*, on my office bookshelf.

I do a circle in the car and take some more photos. You have to go to a place even if you know you have no hope of success. Failure is context, indifference is revealing. The security van does another slow drive-by. I start the engine and move on.

Brandon swings through the automatic doors and eagerly picks up the Coke I've ordered for him, pulling a copy of the local paper out of his pocket and slapping it down on the laminate plastic table. He's 23 years old, the name of the electricians he works for sewn into his polo shirt in the tell-tale medium-res autostitch of workwear wholesalers. He's part of the front-page splash, standing solemnly in his garden with the Mossmorran stacks burning in the background.

He apologises for the confusion – there are three branches of McDonald's in Dunfermline and he didn't specify exactly which. It's not certain this is the legacy of American business Andrew Carnegie envisaged when he started sending money back to Scotland to enrich his home town. We're in the drive-through branch on the edge of the enticingly named Dunfermline Leisure Park, sandwiched between the motorway and acres of newbuild suburban homes. Brandon's van is squeezed into the parking bays next to a poorly tended ornamental hedge. Boy racers circulate slowly around our little identikit bungalow, hunting for parking spaces in order to run in for milkshakes and cheeseburgers. Brandon is an experienced spark who jumped straight into the trades aged 15. He's got more life in him than your average university graduate in their late twenties, speaking like the older guys who've trained him on the job.

Fife is otherwise known as the Kingdom, once the centre of the Scottish state and the home of royalty. It has its own particular dialect, lacking the whine that comes in as you head west, and with firmer consonants than some of the Glasgow accents. It hangs on stubbornly in the former mining towns and farming villages around Dunfermline and Kirkcaldy. You can usually tell a Fifer by the liberal use of the 'eh' at the end of sentences inviting you to nod in agreement, but it doesn't travel. People who move out to study or work essentially become bi-dialectical, code-switching just like the Gaels do in the islands.

'The plant's always had an aura, like', Brandon says, dwelling on what that actually means. As long as Brandon has been alive, so has the plant. Mossmorran's presence isn't just the flare, it's also the drone of industrial equipment at night and the floodlights shining across the fields around. Under the stars it looks like a moonbase, marooned in the unlit black landscape.

From the perimeter fence of the plant the nearest houses are visible across the valley; the last few streets in the towns of Cowdenbeath and Lochgelly – including Brandon's – face the stacks of the facility. They were once mining communities both, just like Kirkcaldy. When Thatcher's second government proceeded with its closures of nominally unprofitable pits the Fife coal belt became a wasteland.

In a cautionary lesson for decarbonisation, the government pushed people into an open labour market and withdrew financial and political support for key industries before they could adapt or reskill. According to the theories of labour that dominated the Thatcher programme, the unemployed in places like Kirkcaldy and Cowdenbeath would be motivated to retrain and seek work, and new industries would arise on the back of technological innovation and market freedom. The labour surplus would also attract companies to the area, it was said. Some of the gulf was filled by the growth of the electronics industry, a band of factories running across the country known as the Silicon Glen making microchips, watches, cash machines and semiconductors. The only problem was that, just like in Airdrie, the Silicon Glen was doomed by the rise of the Asian manufacturing sector and the lack of loyalty shown by investors once profits looked threatened. New rounds of strikes followed as China, Vietnam and Korea offered cheaper labour and quicker delivery.

Adam Smith saw globalisation and free trade as a path to progress, and his disciples pushed deregulation and the removal of trade barriers as a cure for all ills. Confronted with the societal pushback to a decade of economic reform in Scotland, Thatcher gave a speech to the Scottish Conservative

Party in which she claimed that the Scots invented Thatcherism long before she was thought of. A lot of people in Fife wish Thatcher had never been thought of at all.

Mossmorran opened in 1985, run by Shell and Exxon. Under the new energy and industrial regime of the 1980s the petrochemicals industry was allowed to operate without government interference, with sympathetic tax regimes and a dogmatic belief that there was no responsibility to anyone but growth. Both companies are estimated to have spent over a billion dollars on lobbying against clean energy and climate science since the early 1990s. The plant produces ethylene, which is used to make polythene, one of the most commonly used plastics in the world, one of the hardiest and one of the most polluting. Some researchers even argue that plastic waste is as big a threat as climate change. However you see it, they both stem from an enduring love affair with oil and gas.

If you want to understand a society one of the best ways to do it is to look at how it powers itself, and oil is the basic currency of consumer capitalism. Petroleum is light enough that it can be carried around with relative ease but contains enough energy that it can move its own weight and the thing carrying it. It still has huge energy losses of up to 70 per cent in modern cars, but that loss is carried by the consumer and not by the provider. Electricity has the opposite problem. Electric motors are hugely more efficient than petrol engines, yet electricity can't just be carried around. Subways have electric feeder rails, long-distance trains need power lines strung out for hundreds of miles. Petroleum is individualistic energy, the great liberator.

'I think if people realised the amount of money that was being brought in and shifted down they'd react', Brandon says when I ask about the plant and its effects. People around

Mossmorran have for years reported fatigue, childhood sickness and disrupted sleep due to constant activity and flaring. Not long after I meet Brandon there are stories of a string of local cases of blood cancer in the surrounding villages. Strange smells come and go, but the owners remain tight-lipped. Local social-media groups trade experiences and lobby politicians to lean on the energy giants. Usually the reply to the local residents and the environmental regulator is that things are all within legal limits, which is not the same as being harmless.

Dislike of the plant is not just about what it does, but the psychology too. Oil rigs are out of sight and out of mind, but the onshore gas plant is there when people go to bed and there when they wake. 'Half the people in Cowdenbeath dinnae even ken what it's for', says Brandon.

Brandon's stepdad was a kitchen porter at the plant, a job he didn't enjoy but a job nonetheless in a place where good, stable employment is hard to find.

'I think everyone in the family is after something', Brandon says. 'Well, not the youngest actually, he's just born', he adds, chuckling to himself. 'He's no looking for work quite yet.'

Adam Smith believed that wages would grow in line with economic growth and output, but since the 1970s working people have seen an increasingly small return for their work relative to the size of the economy. Owning is far more profitable than working, and social mobility is increasingly chimeric for the children and grandchildren of the baby boom. A journalist friend originally from Scotland's coal country who had been drawn to London by the promise of jobs and exposure glibly lamented to me over coffee that you get depressed about flat wages and no hope of owning a home, but then you see an advertisement for something you like on social media and comfort yourself with an Amazon purchase, knowing that three oligarchs control your life far more than the Church did most of your ancestors.

Just over the motorway from where we sat is an Amazon fulfilment centre. The warehouse is often the first point of call for people looking for work in Fife. Nobody stays long at the fulfilment centres – the recruitment process is the modern equivalent of foremen going to street corners with a list of how many stevedores or bricklayers they need that day. Everything is streamlined and micromanaged, people with lives and minds made as efficient as the conveyors and automated forklifts they pass parcels to and from. The warehouses have thrived in areas of post-industrial Britain where wages are depressed and employment is precarious, but politicians love the logistics companies because they ostensibly create jobs that move people off dependency on the welfare system and improve growth statistics. Some sociologists of technology argue that it is value neutral, and that whether it is good or bad depends on who is in charge. Others think it can be inherently oppressive, and the less critical see it merely as a blunt tool of progress that needs to be accelerated as fast as possible. At the other end of the supply chain from Dunfermline, in Chinese warehouses, different workers with different masters load crates onto trains for shipment to Europe, and money that does not really exist flows from plastic credit cards to pay for plastic hair straighteners, power tools and fast fashion.

For a while, the University of Glasgow had two buildings named after Adam Smith. One was home to sociologists and political scientists, the other to the university Business School. Eventually the Business School won and the sociologists were downgraded to a building with a more prosaic name at the same time as being reorganised by a team of highly paid external consultants.

The Adam Smith Business School is designed to feel like a tech HQ, a multi-floor atrium with exposed concrete and open-plan studios where students can spark one another's entrepreneurial spirit. Someone has set up a branded photo wall where students can photograph themselves to let everyone else know they are in the business of success. At reception, videos play on a loop, telling the story of Smith's explanation of markets and specialisations. In the university gift shop you can buy Adam Smith tote bags along with a Lord Kelvin stationery set. Every ancient university has its own Disney castle that it uses to attract students, buildings ancient and modern that go on every brochure. Lord Kelvin and Adam Smith are Glasgow's Mickey and Minnie Mouse.

One day on my way to a meeting I am accosted by a group of confused Japanese tourists looking for the office in which Adam Smith worked. I explain that the huge brutalist edifice housing the Sociology department was built two hundred years too late. The most famous person to ever work in the building was probably Yannis Varoufakis, the radical Greek economist who lectured in Political Economy at Glasgow in the 1990s and emerged as one of the foremost critics of austerity politics in Europe after the 2008 financial crisis. There are no Varoufakis T-shirts or books on sale in the gift shop, but then the money here is not made in Greece or Scotland, but in London, New York, San Francisco and Shenzhen.

When the world came close to complete economic melt-down in 2008, however, it was not just the result of cartoon capitalists on Wall Street and in the City of London; it was a collapse made in Edinburgh and Glasgow by a Scottish financial class high on its own supply. By the time banks started to default one by one off the back of bad debt and a property crisis in the US, the Edinburgh-headquartered Royal Bank of Scotland had ballooned to become the world's biggest company by assets. Most people on the street had no idea, but the RBS was hours from running out of money before it was bailed out by the UK government.

In the space of a few weeks £133 billion was sunk into four major banks to keep them stable. Kirkcaldy's other famous son, Prime Minister Gordon Brown, helped to coordinate the packages that saved the global financial system, working with the central banks of major economies and European Central Bank to preserve capitalism as we know it, for better or worse.

Like the oil industry, RBS put Scotland on the map and made it into something bigger than its five million people merited. The bank also financed billions in development loans to the oil industry to open up new wells, extending a generous arm of credit to fossil prospectors. When RBS collapsed something broke in the nation's soul. People began to realise that the good news story they had been sold about the best small country in the world was ephemeral, dependent on money that never really existed. A whole generation found their future had been pulled from under their feet, and they never got it back.

Brown is still a well-known face locally, now in his early seventies. He makes the occasional public appearance and reads avidly – he sent one of my and Ewan's colleagues a note saying how much he liked his book about the Fife coal miners.

There's a café by the beach on the Fife coast where Brown sits with his security detail, trying as much as possible to blend in. I found him there one day by chance on the way home from an interview, looking out across the water. I wanted to go over and ask him what it was like in those long hours when everything hung on hastily arranged back-room meetings and transatlantic phone calls, when it seemed that total collapse was inevitable. The collective memory has obscured the facts of the situation, blaming excessive government spending and a bloated welfare state. Everything since has flowed from that moment, as we circle back round for another run at making the same mistakes. I left him be.

Just down the shore from the café is a pier for the petro-chemical tankers that pump the oil from the pipelines running through the landscape, bobbing gently on the slow tide. Over it all the burning tower of Mossmorran lights up the night sky in the name of freedom.

11

In the oil graveyard

It's just approaching 5am when I roll the car to a stop and
turn off the engine in the side road of a housing estate on
the shores of the Firth of Forth. I dim the lights so as not
to attract the attention of the police and rustle around by
phone-torch for my keys and notebook. On the seat beside
me is a yellow vest with PRESS printed in large type on the
back, and I have both my journalism card and university ID
on a lanyard around my neck as insurance.

With the engine stopped and heater off the car is cold – I
don't trust the battery to last long without the motor running
since it died on me in Orkney – and I shiver a little in the
damp. I'm at sea level and the air is moist in the pre-dawn
moments, clinging to the creeks that flow out through the
gap between the docks and the oil refinery in Grangemouth.
I'm in the right place and believe I have the right time, but
the instructions were necessarily vague. I have never actually
met the person who gave them to me, a number sent from
another number on an encrypted messaging app through a
personal referral.

Seven hours before I'd been lying in bed when my phone
buzzed. The text was short. 'Get to the main gate at Ineos,
there'll be something happening after five.' And so here I

am, freezing with the lights off in the glow of one of the biggest petrochemical processing sites in Europe.

The message had been sent by *This is Rigged*, the same direct action collective who'd been occupying fossil-fuel sites around Scotland for the past year or so and posting their manifesto around the university. The police had stepped up security nationwide, but nobody knew where the next action would happen. You can't watch every petrol station, truck stop and fuel-storage depot.

When it happens it comes quick, to the point I barely make it out of the car to get a look. A people carrier pulls up the approach road to the security barriers, looking like a taxi bringing someone in for the start of the morning shift, but it stops short of the gate. Out pile five or so people, who then immediately begin running towards the entrance without looking around. This is the fourth time in two weeks they've hit the plant, concentrating their fire on the entrance where road tankers and the plant workers come and go.

They're met by a line of police officers who pin them to the ground before they can make it past the security booth and padlock themselves to the fence. It's an efficient and well-honed operation; before I can ask any questions they're funnelled into vans and herded off to the local police station a few streets away. I'm left standing in the dawn rain, witness to the latest round of trench warfare between an increasingly well-organised and committed climate movement on one side, and the riot officers of Scotland's police service on the other.

Grangemouth is not just a place, but a landscape in itself, what anthropologists who have written about oil call a *petro-paysage* or *petropolis*. Where the Firth of Forth narrows as it transitions into a river draining from the Highland foothills, Grangemouth dominates the southern shore, a whole ecosystem of steaming pipes and towers occupying what were once wide tidal mudflats and wetlands.

The town is older than oil, growing up around the quayside where the canal from Glasgow met the waters of the east coast. Dominated by the refinery and a deep-water container port that also imports and exports products to the plant, the world flows through Grangemouth – cheap East Asian electronics, Bangladeshi clothes, furniture in containers from Central Europe, and the oil and gas that has sustained the town for decades. The refinery is a body without a face. The security fence that runs for kilometres around its edge is broken every so often by checkpoints and – since the occupations kicked off – police cars. It's what systems engineers call a single point of failure – stop Grangemouth and you stop oil all over the country.

I wander over to the police vans and flash my ID, joined by a photographer from the local newspaper who's been hauled out of his bed to document the latest infraction. There's a liaison officer who steps forward, paid to say very little. The police don't tell me a great deal and nor do I expect them to. The people involved will already be in holding cells at the police station on the main road from Grangemouth to the plant, and once their lawyers arrive they'll be moved to interview rooms, going through a prearranged script for which they've been trained. They do it knowing full well they could end up in prison.

Protesting against climate change is not illegal, but the activists are brought up before the court on a range of public order offences or for causing criminal damage. Most of them are young, in their late teens or early twenties. They have grown up with climate change as a fact of life and as a problem mainstream politics seems unable to solve. The group believes the system is fundamentally rigged in favour of the rich and the large energy companies. Grangemouth is owned by Ineos, a multinational giant belonging to Jim Ratcliffe, co-owner of Manchester United and one of Britain's richest men, and the Chinese state oil company Petrochina.

The activists' demands are straightforward, if ambitious – a complete exit for Scotland from fossil production and a rapid shift away from oil-dependent technologies, along with a redistribution of the amassed wealth to society's most vulnerable. To their detractors the members of the collective are spoiled middle-class kids with better things to be doing with their lives. To the climate movement they are heroes, risking damage to their careers to do what they see as absolutely necessary. Some chain themselves to oil trucks and refineries; some walk around the city spraying 'This Is Rigged' on derelict buildings, making posters and communicating with their public on social media. Others provide legal advice, make sure there's bail money, and find willing drivers with large cars for the occupation drops. There are no clear leaders and members don't even know much about the people acting at the other end of the chain.

Bertolt Brecht said that petroleum resists the five-act form. He meant that its capacity to create speed and power, its flexibility and its social transformation made writing theatre in the age of oil a radically different proposition. Like everyone else, I've become desensitised to oil; the whirr of the petrol-station gauge is as banal as the timer on the washing machine. There was a brief moment when the price per litre matched the measurements exactly, so that the amount and the bill would tick up in beautiful synchronicity and provide the low-level thrill that we seek as our lives become increasingly conformist and regular.

I have the stench of petroleum on my hands as I head back up the east coast, the last few drops from the pump nozzle dribbling on my fingertips when I pull it out of the fuel cap. Whenever I hear the hiss of hot fumes escape from a near-empty tank and see the light refract through the gas before it dissipates I'm reminded that we're all driving around tiny bombs. The stains on the tarmac in the accident hotspots I pass on my drives north and south are crime scenes where petroleum has done its work, where tourists have forgotten to drive on the left or teenagers out in their first car have wrapped it around a fence post. In Scotland almost three hundred young people – mostly teenage boys not long past their driving test – are killed or seriously injured every year in collisions. When my car rolled off the production line I was a teenager too, and the world was half a degree cooler.

On my way through Aberdeen's maze of roundabouts and mini-motorways I avoid a 50mph collision with a powder-blue Audi coupé that overtakes before cutting across my front and speeding off to the suburbs. I don't catch the plates but it can't be more than a year old, and in Aberdeen the luxury car dealerships still do a brisk trade in spite of the oil cutbacks.

This is my last trip back to Aberdeen, for now at least. I'd come for the first time a decade ago to report on the last oil crisis and the supposed good news of the green transition, when I'd first decided to write a book about it. I drive around looking for somewhere to dump the car so I can do an interview at the harbour office. In the no man's land of car parks and warehouses between the railway station and the port, where the oil supply vessels lay to, is one of the region's biggest food banks. It hands out to anyone who needs them parcels of dried food, home essentials like toothpaste and tampons and advice on how to access government support.

I stick my head inside, finding the door between the Pentecostal churches and car workshops. It's the same now as it was when I came through the first time, pallets of bulk ingredients stacked waiting to be distributed.

Renewables were supposed to have transformed Aberdeen by now. It's there in words I wrote myself on the internet in good faith, just like I believed what I wrote about Obama in Berlin and at climate summits in Iceland and Washington. Between the press releases and the pilot projects the problems are still there, though. The food bank was a good-news story that should never have had to exist, in a city that on paper at least was one of the richest in Europe. When the last oil-price crash hit in the early 2010s after the global financial crisis there were tales of people in luxury cars picking up food parcels from the drop-in and pleading with banks to renegotiate mortgages on million-pound homes they could not afford to sell.

The faces are the same as they were a decade before, local families from the high-rises above the harbour, migrants from the Philippines and West Africa who've worked their way here on boats or as service workers, but also people who once had good well-paid jobs and have been dealt a double blow by unemployment and skyrocketing inflation. Wandering down to the harbour, I get chatting to a medical officer who's just come down the gangway from one of the offshore boats. I ask if there's been a COVID-19 outbreak – there's been a new wave doing the rounds and I'm a bit wary being out. Offshore boats and rigs are perfect conditions for the virus. 'Drug tests', he replies. 'Clean, thankfully.'

Aberdeen has two drug markets, one for the recreational party drugs taken by offshore workers and oil execs, and one for the long-term addicts trapped in cycles of poverty and exclusion. Social deprivation and quick money are a drug dealers' paradise. I think of the helicopter lounge, Stevie and Roger sinking pints and mainlining nicotine, and the guy at the fruit machine rubbing his nose.

The boats that come in and out of Aberdeen are diverse – oil vessels, coastal freighters, ferries in for servicing at the marine engineering yard and large baulk carriers full of wind-turbine blades for installation inland. The harbour is sealed off behind gated checkpoints and wire fences – gone are the days when you could just walk into a port with casual workers and crew – now everyone is security checked and accounted for. An anthropologist I worked with in the US told me how after 11 September every railroad yard and construction site in America became off limits to researchers interested in talking to working people, and with the advent of social media companies began to slap bans on truck drivers, steelworkers and energy technicians to stop them discussing their jobs at all. Many contracts now contain clauses about protecting the company reputation on pain of redundancy. A whole section of everyday life has been made invisible to the passer-by.

I pull on my work boots, baseball cap and a marine jacket and slip in around the end of the quay by the local lifeboat station, heading for the three big offshore supply boats the size of small cruise ships moored in the outer harbour. Early in my career I was given a piece of advice by an experienced journalist who had worked in London and Brussels chasing powerbrokers; act like you're supposed to be there. If anyone asks, claim you're supposed to be there, and if you don't have permission to be there pretend it's their fault and ask who you need to talk to to sort it out. A group of men in high-vis jackets are gathered around a digger pulling sheets

of metal out the ground and they leave me be. I head over
to the gangway of the biggest ship and ask if there's anyone
about, flashing my ID card.

The security guard is receptive; he just works for an arms-
length company that provides watchmen to firms across the
energy industry, and he knows little about the boat he's
guarding or the people he works for. He says he can't let me
on board even to see if anyone is there and willing to talk,
and he retreats back into his plastic booth before producing
a number. 'This is the company; ring them, maybe they'll
help?'

I ring the number, and I am told to send an email. I thank
the guy – in the accent of a naturalised Londoner he says
his name is Erdem – and go on my way.

As the light goes the sky pinkens and I wind up in a pub
between oil tanks and locked gates deep in the roads of the
port, the hidden remains of the old harbour village before
oil came. Two crews are fresh in, one from doing survey
work further south in the North Sea, another from an offshore
supply boat resting up between sorties to the rigs. The barmaid
is giving away free pints of cider and discount lager as it
needs to be drunk up before the pumps are serviced. The
crews are only too happy to oblige, men in company jackets
and branded shirts with the name of their vessel stitched
into the breast pocket opposite the corporate logo. The cider
goes quicker than the conversation, but the conversation
follows the cider. The barmaid fills me in on the upturns
and downturns.

'It's like boom and bust in here; there's nothing, then a
big boat comes in or two and the place is full.' It takes
approximately ninety seconds to reach the bar from the dock
gate. You can get a meal with dessert and a pint of cold lager
and come away with change from twenty pounds. She offers

me another free pint of cider and I explain that my brain won't allow it. I can do without even a tiny hangover in my state. I ask about what happens next.

'It's boats and crews and not oil that keep this place going', she says. It's a different world to the other end of town, where the managerial class sip cocktails in well-curated bars and the golf clubs of Aberdeen's commuter hinterland, living in newbuild villas and large houses built with money made at sea but earned indoors.

I leave the pub and wander back to the city centre, past the closed seaman's church that is one of the last pieces of the old village still intact. It's boarded up but the graveyard is semi-managed, the headstones bearing the names of seamen lost before their time, some more recent than is comfortable. Under a tree between the church porch and the gate is an abandoned holdall. At first I think it must belong to someone sleeping rough, but inside is the flotsam of a contract marine electrician, notebooks with wiring diagrams, spare work shirts and changes of underwear. Where the owner is now is unclear, but a leather diary shows a list of names of east-coast ports – Aberdeen, Peterhead, Grimsby, Tynemouth. The bag is on the same route I am. It was left – I hope – by someone five pints in on their way to the warm shower of one of the budget hotels that sit next to Aberdeen's harbour front and industrial parks.

The company that owns the boat has got back in touch, via a press officer in the Netherlands and a subsidiary in London. I'm sent a list of statistics with information on how much energy the boat has saved through smart sailing, how it uses a hybrid battery system to stop air pollution and noise on the port, and what it is capable of lifting. I email back to ask if I could speak to anyone about what goes on inside the boats, and a reply pings back in a tone different from the language of reputation management and press releases. Another interview I'd set up the same day collapses, a friend of a friend in a drilling firm who was happy to talk but backed out when their HR compliance officer got wind of it.

Eventually I find myself five miles inland in a business park on the edge of the city where it meets the farmland of Aberdeenshire, looking at a row of model ships in glass cabinets just like the one in the harbour. These are neat three-storey offices bearing the company emblem replete with coffee stations and shielded meeting rooms off the open-plan floor. It reminds me of a newsroom, albeit with less pressure to pump out the product.

This is the other end of the oil industry, a long way from the helicopter passengers in their survival suits going on and off rigs, or the crane operators lifting equipment onto the supply boat decks. Up here in the suburbs and business parks, in well-heated offices lit by LED lights and serviced by invisible cleaners, sit the analysts, the accountants, the technical planners, the PR people and the engineers. These are not oil jobs in the normal sense, but jobs that depend on oil, in an economy formed by oil. The industrial area where the offices are located is a jigsaw of car parks and low-rise offices linked by roundabouts and surrounded by petrol stations and trunk roads. Pride of place is given to the campus of the French oil company Total, and around about, in more architecturally limited buildings, is an eco-system of hangers-on and service providers.

In reception I look at the headed notepaper and the signed Aberdeen FC football in a case on the coffee table – the company that owns the boats is one of the club sponsors and the football club's mixed fortunes mirror that of the industry. The oil money has not made them perpetual champions but instead flowed elsewhere and paid for teams in the English Premier League to achieve unparalleled success. When he bought part of Manchester United, Jim Ratcliffe wanted a marquee football club to go with his Monaco home and ballooning personal wealth. Aberdeen were not on his shopping list.

Paul is the one who sent me the email. He's from the Shire, as locals call the area beyond the city, the hinterland of farming communities and small towns that stretches out from the coast up into the Grampian mountains. He'd done his time away working overseas as a marine engineer before coming home to start a family.

'Seventy per cent of what we do is decom', he says matter-of-factly about the realities of the industry. The days of sinking new wells and constant prospecting are over, and though there is more oil and gas out there it is not necessarily worth going after. Instead the focus is on raising the relics of the past, sealing old wells, and where possible bringing old rigs in for deconstruction. The North Sea is going through a mini-decommissioning boom as production rigs come offline and companies try to meet their legal obligations and recover anything that might be too valuable to leave behind. One of the world's most intensively exploited oil and gas fields needs someone to sweep up afterwards.

'We've been very busy with renewables too', he says more optimistically. The oil supply vessels are also well suited to supporting wind farms, carrying turbine blades and service equipment to the hundreds of turbines springing up along the east coast. 'We're an oil and gas company; we're here to support the oil and gas industry, but we're always looking at other opportunities.' He tells me about new tech for diver-less cable-laying technology the company is working on.

Hidden in Paul's point is the same larger truth about life after oil that is obvious anywhere you go in Scotland. Green energy simply doesn't create as many jobs as oil and gas. Whereas a single oil rig might have two hundred people on board, automation and the lower risk of renewables themselves means there is less and less need for living, breathing people to be out at sea, and less enthusiasm for the inherently dangerous work that comes with moving volatile hydrocarbons from pockets under the seabed. The trickle-down model of oil wealth where companies make big profits and people pick up large crumbs simply cannot hold. Like in Shetland, where the huge turbines need just a handful of people to watch over them, or in Caithness, where the poverty is barely concealed beyond the harbour access roads, something is missing. In Aberdeen public libraries are closing, the local health board is dealing with a seventy-million-pound shortfall, and the coming end of the carbon economy is making people realise that the promises of the new energy revolution could be as hollow as the bed of the North Sea.

I'm packing for a conference trip to Stavanger, Norway's oil capital and Aberdeen's alternate reality where the money flowed back to the public, when I hear the news.

Grangemouth is closing, the jobs are going, and the oil refinery is winding down. The whole operation could be gone within as little as a year. I ring Ewan, who has an inside track with the trade unions, and ask what's happened.

He's diplomatic but invites me to a protest march at the plant. 'There's a lot to see', he says on the phone. This is less a victory for the climate-change protesters than a capitulation to the whim of the oil multinationals.

When I get to the east coast, the car park of the Grangemouth Stadium is slowly filling with people, unsure what

to expect but hoping for something. The numbers are out
and four hundred local people will lose their jobs. The trade
unions have said the knock-on effects with local supply
chains could impact three thousand workers. Someone is
handing out T shirts and reflective jackets saying NO BAN
WITHOUT A PLAN on the back. I take one from the cardboard box and stick it in my bag.

Less than six months before I had sat in a university lecture
hall watching an Ineos executive boast about the plant's
green credentials at a round table. The official line to poli-
cymakers and climate researchers had been that the emissions
from the plant were a small price to pay for the employment
it created, pointing to the low carbon footprint compared to
terminals in Nigeria and the Far East where regulation was
slacker. The people behind the wire fence turned out to be
entirely disposable when it came down to it.

The march is hastily arranged, but the turnout is decent
enough. It sets off led by a colliery band from a local coal
mine that no longer exists, five hundred people doing a loop
around the centre of Grangemouth from the athletics track
to the town park. We pass the Ineos offices and the cooling
towers and pipework of the plant itself to make some noise.
It's a protest in name only. It feels more like a New Orleans
funeral procession.

The string of marchers is made up of unlikely fellow-
travellers; a former leader of the Scottish Labour Party,
independence campaigners, plant workers, environmentalists
and socialist activists waving their respective flags. Behind
the scenes, all the main political parties merely favour a
more humane form of asset management by private capital
when all is said and done, but they still make sure to turn
out and reassure people they are fighting tooth and nail for
their future come election time.

Ewan is there, marching with one of his PhD students who's been interviewing the plant workers, and familiar faces I know from Friends of the Earth and a few other climate NGOs. Some have come up from London, a whole busload across from Glasgow, and many from the end of the road. At an upstairs window two men wave as the parade passes, and Gillian, a member of parliament for the Green Party who was born and raised on the streets around the plant, waves back. It's her dad.

'It's his birthday the day', she chuckles. 'Once I'm done here I've to go round and do the cake.'

Until the spring Gillian's party had been in government, part of a coalition that had made big promises about decarbonisation and economic reform in the public interest. What looked like a progressive front had turned sour as Scotland was forced to admit it was going to miss its world-leading climate targets, and instead of trying to catch up, the money men had asserted themselves. The Greens were cast off to try and steady the declining fortunes of the nationalist government and the country took a few steps backwards on climate.

The closure of Grangemouth is a foretaste of what could happen to the rest of the fossil industry as owners pull out and economise. Scotland is on the verge of systematic economic failure if it isn't careful.

Gillian now has four hundred more unemployed people to lobby for in parliament, alongside making sure that the town isn't just cast by the wayside. 'We've got to have a just transition', she shouts over the noise as we walk. 'Just shutting down oil doesn't work.'

Then I catch sight of a sign in the crowd, poster paint on cardboard. It's This Is Rigged, or some of them at least. The people I saw bundled into police vans in the early dawn are absent, in custody or on bail and forbidden from contact with the broader movement. Many of the group are banned from attending demonstrations as part of their sentencing. These are new faces but they wear the same uniform, bob haircuts or shaved heads and second-hand jackets, boots and jeans. I go over and ask how they feel about having their wishes granted.

'This isn't what we wanted or what we asked for,' they say despairingly. The protests were designed to spearhead new investment in publicly owned green technology, not to throw the people who work in the plant under the bus. 'They're just going to ship these emissions overseas', another of the marchers says. I ask if they're going to carry on running their direct-action campaigns.

'Absolutely.'

The march reaches the park and the crowd thins out. People break off into groups. Speeches are made, manifestos delivered, and the question of what happens next hangs in the air without being answered. I turn and look at the chimneys of the plant venting steam into the sky and the town made in their image below. It isn't clear where Scotland goes now, but something has to give. Oil is over.

12

Future poems

I wake up looking at the last of the night as it vanishes above me. On the cliffs the buzzards circle in the dawn. I'm not in my bed. My first thought is for coffee and I sit up, glancing around for the kettle. It must be somewhere between four and five A.M. , based on the strength of the light.

I pull myself off the deck of the bothy and go inside to push the button on the gas canister and spark the hob. The water boils, hot North Sea gas transferring heat to metal and metal to water until the spout whistles. It's time to leave.

As the coffee kicks in I wonder if it will be a good or a bad day for my brain, apprehensive about driving. The car is dumped round the back of the port buildings on the mainland, waiting for the boat to bring me home from the dreamworld I have been living in.

Remembering how to be awake and lucid is the hardest. I had sat up the night before on a bed of blankets, watching out for the birds of prey on the thermals behind the bothy. The twilight over the Atlantic had turned into a slow-moving window on the universe. I don't remember falling asleep, save the stars being there one minute and the buzzards in the dawn the next. There's dew on my hair but the morning is warm and I don't shiver. The bracken forms a curtain so nobody can see me, and I take a shower outside under the solar-heated tank. From the front of the bothy I have a perfect view of the sea all the way out to South Uist. The Atlantic is deceptively calm.

The little cube building I am in uses sustainable firewood, solar-heated water and compost wastewater. It is so well insulated that you have to open the door before you go to bed so you don't cook yourself alive in your sleep if the stove is on. It was built as a proof of concept for sustainable small living, five by four metres, with everything you could need for an ascetic and aesthetically curated existence. Now it's rented out by a charity to artists and writers looking for space to work. On the bookshelf inside is a consciously chosen canon of nature writing. Nan Shepherd brushes shoulders with Thoreau, contemporary eco-poets and coffee-table adventurers, alongside birding books and geological compendia of the Hebrides.

The view from the houses around the bay supposedly inspired Tolkien's visions of Mordor, peaks ringed by cloud picked out black against a rolling sky. Looking out at the summits of Askeval and Hallival, island peaks named by the Vikings across the water on Rúm, I am in a pocket universe, where the view hasn't changed in the millennium since the Norwegian kings colonised the west.

Eigg is one of the small isles, a chain of four main islands just off the west coast of the Scottish mainland underneath Skye. They are all unique, with different shapes and histories. Canna, furthest out, is long and flat. Rúm is all mountains, emptied of people and run as a government nature reserve, Muck is diminutive and owned by a single family, and Eigg is divided neatly in two by a ridge of rock with long linear settlements on either side, owned collectively by the people who live there.

Like the Mhoine crofters, Eigg was purchased from an absentee landlord in the 1990s, one of the first victories of Scotland's land-reform movement. In a decade it went from an anachronism of crumbling buildings lacking basic infrastructure into a community-run, low-carbon lab of self-build houses and small businesses with a population of a hundred. People now pay good money to come for the week, to see a model society in action.

Eigg is no paradise – living here means working hard and a major adjustment to a drastically different way of life. People who come merely to escape their problems often find themselves presented with a new set, just as the incomers in Shetland and Orkney do. The dream of leaving modernity behind and building a cleaner, simpler version is enticing, though, whatever your reasons. In the harbour café the same conversation is repeated a thousand times between the residents and the visitors. Londoners, Dutch, Germans, French and Glaswegians all read from the same script. How did you end up coming here? It's so peaceful, isn't it? I wish I could stay forever. Did you see the dolphins? You must be so happy living in such a wild place. Is the weather always this nice?

Getting back to nature has become an increasingly lucrative business; the eco-retreat has allowed us to pretend for a moment that we can be different people to the ones who stare back at us in the mirror each morning. The first time I came to this place was to write about it for a magazine, and it stuck in my dreams, not just the view across the open Atlantic out over the peaks and sea cliffs, but the sense of emancipation from everything else. No more being chased for student debt repayments or struggling to pay the heating bill, and most recently, liberation from the dead weight of illness. As my brain tried to rewire itself I returned to this cabin in my imagination again and again – for whatever reason, my subconscious settled on the western flank of Eigg a place of safety, something to aim for in the darker moments.

As I pour the coffee from the pot and stare out at the view, the reality and the anticipation meet for the last time. Neurons start to fire, and I look to the writing desk where my computer sits next to the radio recorder with the interviews from the road, lodged on the memory cards and in three large notebooks. I take the first gulp and the world hardens a little and gains form.

Scholars of science and technology call dreamscapes of the future a sociotechnical imaginary. It's a place ever present but always just out of view where we project our dreams and nightmares. Now and then we catch a glimpse, and a few of us get to live it, but most of us end up with a kind of diluted and bastardised version moulded by circumstance.

We know that the imaginary is just that; the real problem is that the reality we inhabit is equally illusory. The world we think we live in is already dead. The tragedy of climate change is that there is no mystery to any of it – we understand perfectly what is going on and the challenge is in breaking the collective delusion that we can somehow carry on as we have done for the past half-century.

Thatcher's children were supposed to inherit a world already on the path to transformation; we fully believed that by the time we were adults things really could only get better. This was our first shared dreamscape, but the temporality has changed. Climate change is no longer a future risk to be prevented; it is an ongoing crisis from which we need to escape, yet we cannot just escape to nature. There are no deeper truths to be found here as we walk through the wilderness in search of liberation.

My neurologist thinks that one reason my brain reacted so badly to physical trauma is the nature of my work – an inability to let go and give up, to let life happen around me. When I listen back to recorded conversations from the road one of the pervading emotions is urgency, the other resignation. Do the young climate activists holding Obama HOPE banners fifteen years ago, now pushing forty with the sober knowledge of years visible in their face, still hold that same hope? Somewhere in a file I still have the newspaper cutting of my first-ever front page, an optimistic report about global climate action written for the student newspaper with all the misplaced confidence of a teenager who thinks they are the finished product.

The poetry on the bookshelves in the bothy is precise, sublime and beautiful, and largely devoid of politics. People are afraid of politics even as reality bites, constantly deferring to an imagined objective centre of sensible decisions and consensus over confrontation. Marx talked of the poetry of the future, a form of imagination that was prepared to see the current moment as a transformational epoch, a new language and a reckoning with the old. He argued that the social revolution of the 1800s could never possibly work with the language it had inherited, and today is no different. And so we hunt for the grammar that works, the language and the rhythm of a different kind of society that beats not with the drum of four-stroke engines but with the hum of turbines and the rise and fall of the waves. All of the pieces are there, waiting to be assembled in the right order. Post-carbon society doesn't need anything we don't already possess, but it does need us to see energy as the force that shapes our world and its future, both the energy we produce and the energy we struggle against.

Scotland is where it began, and maybe where it ends too. We helped to build the world of carbon capitalism and now we have to unbuild it. All the wind farms in the country won't so much as dent emissions in China or India, but we have other weapons – technology, experience and wealth. The past has happened, the future will happen, and we sit balanced between the two with delicate agency and the tools in our hands.

Narratologists call it genre, the loose web of expectations about how our lives and the world at large will unfold. Sometimes those expectations are never realised, sometimes they come undone, and they are full of contradictions. Dream homes destroyed by hurricanes, dream holidays that burn jet fuel in the upper atmosphere and put paradise islands beneath the waves, or the desire merely to live well in a world that is structurally rigged against us. We have to constantly reimagine our futures as some hopes fade and others materialise, dancing on the shifting plates of the present.

Burnout and depression are common behind the curtain of professionalism among science journalists and climate researchers. Some are energised by the prospect of salvation; others retreat into themselves. I flit between the two; I have had my future torn apart and rebuilt once; and if there is one positive it is that the slow loosening of the paralysis of illness gives you a new enthusiasm for living. Nothing is stronger than the will to make good use of the path you have left to run.

The protesters locking themselves to the gates of the oil refineries and sitting in police cells waiting to be interviewed think of a future beyond themselves. The crofters contemplating a retreat from the sea want to know who will pay for flood defences and storm drains, and about what will happen to their land as they hand it on to their children. The oil workers facing redundancy and the inhabitants of post-industrial towns think of schools and jobs and better futures. Some ambitions are shared, some are private, but we are all measured against the enormity of the longer forces that move us with their ebb and flow, little lives playing out at a pivotal moment in human history.

The ferry leans slightly as it comes around the edge of the island on its way into the Eigg pier and I wade onto the ramp through the shallows with my kit bag, chucking it in a pile on the open deck next to the sheep trailers. The crew have started to stack the baggage on pallets, and I think about the abandoned holdall in the graveyard in Aberdeen. In that bag was a whole world.

I walk up the steps to the foredeck and haul myself up onto a small ledge under the bridge. The *Loch Nevis* was the last of the West Coast boats to be built this way. My boots dangle over the edge and I lean back into the slope of the forward cabin to make an impromptu deckchair as the safety announcements come over the deck speakers in both languages. Straight ahead are blue skies over the mountains of Lochaber and people look for otters and dolphins in Galmisdale Bay to starboard. There's a low rumble and the tell-tale smell of marine diesel that has followed me for two years; engines start again and we set out in a straight line towards the harbour arm in Mallaig fifteen miles away. The ferry is a speck of red, black and white on a frosted glass plate transiting from one world to another.

The boat gets in to Mallaig and I haul my own world around the harbour to where the car is waiting. I check the mileage clock; I've driven ten thousand miles out and back around Scotland in the space of two summers and two winters, with countless hours of recordings – people talking, oyster-catchers on the low tide, the rumble of deck-loading ramps and oil helicopters, the wind blowing through Glen Affric and the rustle of the trees, jet planes passing overhead on their way to America, and the slow hum of turbines. I have countless sketches and notes. Some are just names and numbers, some are hand-drawn maps, or scribbled stats saying 100MW or .2 to .4 metres rise, confidence intervals for sea levels and storm severity. The glove compartment is littered with used ferry tickets, lunch receipts and parking permits, branded pens from oil companies and museums, empty trays of medication and a pin badge from the Stromness lifeboat station.

We remain on track for between two and three degrees of global warming, and every notch on the scale is a multiplier. Two degrees is bad, three degrees is catastrophic, and as we enter the mid-2020s global average temperatures are making themselves felt for everyone. Heatwaves, droughts, extreme storms and vanishing beaches will become the norm. We are only half-ready, and my thoughts are never far from what is coming down the road: Andrew standing in the wind over Yell in Shetland and the plans for the climate refuges, the empty supermarket shelves and the closed roads in the tidal surges, or the water cascading through the gorge of the River Kelvin and the surging torrent of the Valencia suburbs. I think too about the wildfire smoke in North America, the friend from Brazil enraptured by the pictures of the Hebrides who saw their home city devastated by coastal floods, people struggling in the Japanese heat, and temperature records being tossed casually aside around the world. Climate change is horrific, but energy can be beautiful. This is the poetry of the future.

Energy is the thread that weaves the cloth. An outline for what might be and a lesson in the mistakes of the past, both accidental and by design. There is something real here in Scotland beyond the disappointment of the present and the past, inescapable and enticing. And good.

From Mallaig I drive south and south again for hours. The road from the isles dips in and out of the coast, under and over the railway and past the turning for the Kintail summits and the Last Ent, before they part company for an hour and reunite on the far side of the Nevis range. They track one another through the passes down to Loch Lomond and Glasgow past electric car-charging points and hydro schemes, under the shadow of the Luss Hills and into the lowlands. I cross the Clyde on the motorway, cutting through the city, and carry on into the Lanarkshire coalfields, accelerating on to the high ground around Coalburn and its turbines, solar farms and batteries. I pull up Beattock summit at the top of the borderlands next to the electric trains that rise silently as they lean into the curves, then drop down again towards the sea and the ridges of the Lakeland fells on the horizon over the English border. I am headed for a house on the edge of the fields in a small town in the hills.

Dad has been ill, just in time for his eighth decade. News reached me as I sat in an Aberdeen hotel room after an interview one day, marshalling clips into folders at a fibreboard veneer desk. Every two weeks his body is bombarded with targeted radioactive waves using isotopes manufactured in nuclear reactors, piercing the DNA of the cancer cells and pulling them apart in plastic medical gowns made from the remains of ancient life long dead. The prognosis is good, but I've been driving up and down through southern Scotland to visit the little town in the hills more regularly.

When I arrive the whole family is already there, including my brother and his kids, over from America. The youngest of us is two and the oldest seventy years hence. Dad was born in the shadow of the Second World War and the beginnings of the explosion in carbon and human life that have come to dominate the planet. My niece and nephew might yet see the end of it, a stable climate and a way out eighty years from now. They run around in the garden and play by the river, looking for frogs and watching the trains trundle across the fields over the back wall.

We do what families do, we talk and don't talk, we sit out on the steps and we eat ice cream that dribbles down our chins in sticky waterfalls as it meets the sun. The dog roams the house, making sure everyone is present and correct before returning to her blanket for another sleep. I stand alone in the back garden looking over the wall at the sheep between the house and the railway line, thinking.

My niece comes out from the kitchen, jumping down the step onto the gravel. She catches her balance and stands up straight before brushing her hands on her knees. She spies me and waves hello, wandering over to see what I am doing. I ask if she wants to see the sheep and she nods, so I lift her up and hold her tight to my chest, balancing her feet on the dry stone with our heads pressed together.

She points at the sheep with pure wonder, and my thoughts lift for a few seconds, away from the world and towards the line of her hand and the here and now.

And in that moment we live.